LITTLE VOICE

a screenplay

Mark Herman was born in east Yorkshire in 1954. After
graduating in graphic design at Leeds Polytechnic he went on
to study at the National Film School in Beaconsfield.
Following *Blame it on the Bellboy* and *Brassed Off*, *Little Voice*
is his third feature as both writer and director.

LITTLE VOICE

a screenplay by
Mark Herman

based on the stage play
THE RISE AND FALL OF LITTLE VOICE *by*
Jim Cartwright

Methuen Film

Published by Methuen 1999

1 3 5 7 9 10 8 6 4 2

First published in Great Britain in 1999
by Methuen Publishing Limited
20 Vauxhall Bridge Road, London SW1V 2SA

Random House Australia (Pty) Limited
20 Alfred Street, Milsons Point, Sydney, New South Wales 2061, Australia
Random House New Zealand Limited
18 Poland Road, Glenfield, Auckland 10, New Zealand
Random House South Africa (Pty) Limited
Endulini, 5A Jubilee Road, Parktown 2193, South Africa

Methuen Publishing UK Limited Reg. No. 3543167

A CIP catalogue record for this book is available from the British Library

Papers used by Methuen Publishing Ltd are nautral, recyclable products
made from wood grown in sustainable forests. The manufacturing processes
conform to the enviromental regulations of the country of origin.

ISBN 0 413 73490 0

Typeset by MATS, Southend-on-Sea, Essex
Printed and bound in Great Britain by
Cox & Wyman Ltd, Reading, Berkshire

INTRODUCTION

The first time I saw the stage production of Jim Cartwright's
The Rise and Fall of Little Voice I was totally bowled over but
thought there was absolutely no way it could be made into a
film. Watching the same production, film producer Elizabeth
Karlsen was also totally bowled over, but thought there was
absolutely no way it *couldn't* be made into a film. Which only
goes to show a) my non-dislike of the double negative and b)
Elizabeth's and my relative abundance and dearth of
perception.

A few years later, having completed *Brassed Off* and
steadily tearing my hair out trying to think of a follow-up,
Elizabeth asked me if I fancied adapting and directing a film
version of *Little Voice*. With baldness being the only option, I
had to accept. I actually accepted because of the challenge –
all elements that I thought prohibited the play from becoming
a film could now simply become problems to solve. Manna
from Heaven for the masochistic screenwriter. I suppose the
biggest challenge was to prevent the film from feeling stage-
bound, as so often happens with screen adaptations of plays.
This was particularly difficult with a piece that is
fundamentally about a girl who never leaves her bedroom
which, even taking into account the wallpaper, is hardly
cinematic. Moulding an overtly and splendidly theatrical
piece so that it is accessible to a movie audience (and with it,
a movie intelligence) is a very intricate affair. It is not simply
a question of pictorially opening out a story that is basically
interior, which this one undoubtedly is, but in total a massive

balancing act – playing with time, mood, character, language and plot whilst simultaneously trying as hard as one can to protect and stay truthful to the original work. Ironically, while I was busy taking these awful liberties with Jim's play, somebody else was busy rewriting *Brassed Off* for the stage.

While I strongly believe you can't make a good film from a bad screenplay, I think it is all too possible to make a bad film from a good one. There is a huge minefield between page and screen and you need a cast and crew of enormous talent and energy if you are going to reach the other side in anything like good shape.

Mark Herman
October 1998

Opening credits over black. Quiet opening music is undermined by a deeply unattractive snore. Fade up to:

INT. MARI'S BEDROOM. HOUSE. DAY.
Morning light from the window floods into the room. The camera tracks past a dangling hand with garishly painted fingernails and up an arm to the source of the snore: a lump of duvet. The camera continues to creep gently, peacefully, in towards the bed. As we reach it, suddenly, the huge, heftily trumpeted opening and booming vocals of:

> *'Come Fly With Me' – by Frank Sinatra*

. . . which shakes us as much as it shakes the house. It certainly shakes the hell out of MARI. *She springs up, her face as crumpled as her sheets, even more hung-over than she is into her knackered forties. A second ago in the Land of Nod, now she doesn't know what bloody country she's in. She yells, but for* MARI *this morning, a yell is like a hatchet to the top of the head.*

MARI: Oh, for ff . . . *LV!!*
SOUNDTRACK: *Come fly with me let's fly, let's fly away*
                    If you can use some exotic booze there's a bar
                            in far Bombay . . .

INT. LITTLE VOICE'S BEDROOM. DAY.
LV *is oblivious to her mother's shout. She is in her late twenties but, in her childlike manner and dress, she seems strangely stuck in her early teens. Lit by the morning light through the window of*

1

*her peculiarly shaped loft room, she stands, totally enveloped in
the Sound of Sinatra, her arms stretched out sideways as she, too,
'floats down to Peru'. Opening title:*

LITTLE VOICE

*as the camera tracks back amid this sea of volume to reveal a
bedroom floor carpeted with seemingly hundreds of old record
sleeves, indeed a whole bedroom devoted to a massive collection.
Many smiles from many faces from many eras beam up:
Garland, Bassey, Monroe, Dietrich, Fitzgerald, Holiday etc. On
the only blank wall, almost shrine-like, is a single framed
photograph of a* MAN. *His smile is less showbizzy, more genuine
than the ones on the album covers. He stares out from the frame
with friendly loving eyes.*

SOUNDTRACK: *Come fly with me, let's fly, let's fly away,
Come fly with me let's float down to Peru,
in llama-land there's a one-man band
and he'll toot his flute for you
Come fly with me, let's take off in the blue . . .*

INT. HALLWAY. HOUSE. DAY.
The crashing and joyful swing of Sinatra seems out of place with
MARI*'s morning ritual: the struggle to surface and the seemingly
futile attempts to make herself look half decent. She goes from
bedroom to bathroom and back, never straightening from a stoop.*

SOUNDTRACK: *Once I get you up there where the air is
rarefied,
We'll just glide, starry-eyed . . .*
MARI: Oh, *LV!!* Will you *shut that UP!*

INT. LITTLE VOICE'S BEDROOM. DAY.

Credits continue as LV *is also going through her morning ritual: carefully, meticulously, cleaning and replacing records in their sleeves. Reading the cover notes on one of the sleeves, she leaves the bedroom and heads downstairs . . .*

SOUNDTRACK: *Once I get you up there, I'll be holding you so near*
You may hear, angels tear, 'cos we're together.
Weather-wise it's such a lovely day . . .

EXT. PIGEON HILL. DAY.

We see several dozen pigeons circling in the sky above. Looking up at them from his pigeon shack on a hill above the harbour is the good (but shy-looking) BILLY, *who looks out of place here in his British Telecom overalls. He smiles into the sky and starts to wave a tatty flag, rattle food, and whistle them in.*

SOUNDTRACK: *. . . just say the words and we'll beat the birds down to Acapulco Bay.*
It's perfect for a flying honeymoon they say.
Come fly with me, let's fly, let's fly away.

INT. KITCHEN. HOUSE. DAY.

LV *enters the kitchen, fills the kettle and, wary of the socket overloaded with plugs, very tentatively turns it on at the mains. She opens the fridge door to be initially repelled but finally brave enough to extract a bottle of milk. The milk is solid. She puts it to one side.*

INT. FRONT ROOM. HOUSE. DAY.

As the raunchy trumpet break hits a peak, LV *does a private*

3

dance through to the front room. Behind her, in the hall, MARI
*staggers grumpily towards the bathroom. On her way she turns
and yells at* LV, *pointing upstairs:*

MARI: *LV!! CULL IT!*

EXT. PIGEON HILL. DAY
Now inside the meshed cages, among the many hungry birds,
BILLY *pecks a bird on the head, gives it seed, then hears a beep
and a shout and looks down towards his BT cherry-picker van on
the road below. His elder, stockier co-worker,* GEORGE, *points
with dwindling patience to his watch.* BILLY *nods, and puts the
bird gently back on a perch.*

SOUNDTRACK: *Once I get you up there where the air is
    rarefied
   We'll just glide, starry-eyed
   Once I get you up there I'll be holding you so
    near
   You may hear angels cheer, 'cos we're together*

INT. KITCHEN. DAY.
MARI *comes into the kitchen rattling pills and searching for a cup
or something in the pile of unwashed crockery on the sideboard.
Eventually, with a thump on the bottle-bottom, she empties out
the solid milk, replaces it with water from the tap, drops in the
pills, shakes up the frothy Resolve and swigs it down.*

SOUNDTRACK: *Weather-wise it's such a lovely day
   You just say the words
   and we'll beat the birds down to Acapulco
    Bay
   It's perfect for a flying honeymoon they say*

Come fly with me, let's fly, let's fly . . .
pack up, let's fly away . . .
The kettle boils as the music and credits end. She turns off
the switch and jolts back at a savage, shocking SMACK of
electricity from the groaning collection of plugs.

MARI: Bugger!

EXT. PIGEON HILL. DAY.
BILLY *catches* GEORGE *up as they walk towards the* BT *van.*
He glances at his watch.

GEORGE: Aye, we're late.

Thanks to you and bloody Tweetie Pie back there.

BILLY: Wasn't worrying about work.

Was worrying about Duane.

GEORGE: Duane?

BILLY: Big race today. Setting off from France at nine.

Strong winds forecast.

Doesn't like winds, doesn't Duane.

GEORGE *eyes him with suspicion.*

GEORGE: Duane's . . . a pigeon, right?

BILLY: Aye.

Where're we off?

GEORGE *consults a schedule.*

GEORGE: Shipley Street. Domestic installation.

BILLY *nods. As far as new work partners are concerned,*
GEORGE *reckons he's drawn one of the shorter straws.*

EXT. HOFF HOUSE. SHIPLEY STREET. DAY.
A large, quirky, neglected and unkempt corner block in an
otherwise decent neighbourhood. The faded name on the shop
front: Francis Hoff – Record Exchange – Gramophone Repairs
etc. Above it a bay window leans out at first-floor level, and

above that, a small narrow window at the top of the house. We hear a toilet flush.

INT. HALLWAY. HOUSE. DAY.
In the hallway, GEORGE *is on his hands and knees finishing off the connection while* BILLY, *sitting on the stairs, unwraps a vile, tastelessly garish telephone.* MARI *prowls impatiently around, watching eagerly. Between now and the end of the film, she will hardly ever either stand still or draw breath.*

MARI: Are we nearly done?
　　Ooh, I'll be wired up to the world soon, me, eh?
　　Be in touch with all parts.
GEORGE: Nearly done.
MARI: Goodly.
　　Spend me life and me fortune in them slot boxes, really I do.
　　Ooh, ey, them uniforms are not very becoming.
　　You look like you've been chucked in a tool bag, you.
　　Put me right off, that has.
　　And I always liked a man in a uniform, me.
GEORGE: I bet you did.
MARI: Ey, watch it, Sparks. Sparkeler. *Haar!*
　　Ey, now, speaking of sparks,
　　you don't know nothing about electrickery, do you?
　　The wires of me home is crackling up on me.
GEORGE: No, we're just phone boys, us.
　　MARI *watches handsome, bashful* BILLY.
MARI: Ey, he's quiet, in't he? Is there anybody there?
　　Or has he been disconnected? *Haar!* Eh?
　　Been cut off?
　　I've gorra daughter like that.
　　Like one of them answering thingies.
　　You can only leave messages, like.

6

GEORGE: Say hi, Bill.

BILLY: 'Lo.

MARI: 'Bill?'

Ey, you're not the famous phone bill, are you?

GEORGE *and her laugh – she disproportionately.*

MARI: Oh ey, look at you, though, in that bag.

You ought to complain.

I might phone and complain for you.

Good-looking on the top, then that.

Clark Gable in a bag.

Or should I say Clark *Cable? Haar!*

LV *trots down the stairs, but stops suddenly when she sees* BILLY *and* GEORGE. *She is frozen for a second, shocked by the presence of strangers.* BILLY *stands on the stairs, making way for her. He smiles politely. She half-smiles back, then passes by him and hurries through to the kitchen.* BILLY *watches her go.*

MARI: Ooh, look at them two looking now!

(*Through to* LV:) Ey, this one doesn't speak neither, love.

Could go out you two for a silent night holy night.

LV *comes back into the hall, a handful of Ryvitas.*

MARI: Or stop here and have a bleeding quiet night in.

Be a right riot, that would, eh?

MARI *mimics a zip-lipped, mummified duo.* GEORGE *laughs.* LV, *painfully embarrassed, rushes back upstairs.*

MARI: What did I say? What did I say?

Oh eh, look at the red on him now, looky. Oh dear.

We hear the up-tempo and thunderous opening to a record thud down from above. GEORGE *and* BILLY *are surprised by this behaviour.* GEORGE *embarrassed,* BILLY *intrigued.* MARI *irritated.*

'Come Rain Or Come Shine' – by Judy Garland

MARI: Oh aye, see, that's all you get when she's upset.

Crappity records, full bloody blast . . .
(*Strides to the bottom of the stairs near* BILLY *and shouts up.*)
EY!! YOU!! Trash that calypso!

INT. LITTLE VOICE'S BEDROOM. DAY.
LV *sits next to the record player, her eyes tight closed, madly tapping out the rhythm with her fretful fingers.*

INT. HALLWAY/FRONT ROOM. HOUSE. DAY.
MARI *lights a half-smoked cigarette, takes a drag then stubs it out.*

GEORGE: Right, we're all done.
    I'll just ring through and test the line.
MARI: Oh, let me, go on, lemme lemme.
    She grabs his chunky mobile phone.
    What's 'number again? Oh, wait, I remember . . .
    Taps out the numbers.
    Start of War, and Bobby Moore . . . '39, '66, . . .
    And me age, twenty-eight, what you laughing at, you?
    Her phone rings, shrill. Even the ring is tacky.
MARI: Oh music, music! Ringing in me bloody ears, eh?
    Picks up new phone.
    Hello, me! Haar!

INT. LITTLE VOICE'S BEDROOM. DAY.
LV *sits cross-legged in the middle of her room, very still, staring straight ahead. The camera tracks in on the object of her gaze: the photo of the* MAN, *as Judy gets more frantic, manic, breathless.*

8

I'm gonna love you, I'm gonna love you,
I'm gonna lo-ove you, come rain or come
shine . . .

INT. HALLWAY. HOUSE. DAY.
BILLY*'s attention is drawn more to the noise upstairs than the*
tidying up downstairs. MARI, *waiting by the door, spots him.*

MARI: Barmy, in't it?
Couped up there in the dark all day like a frigging bird
trapped in the rafters.
GEORGE: Steady now, Billy's fond of his birds.
MARI: Aye, well, didn't think he looked like the shirt-lifting
type somehow. *Haar!*
GEORGE: No, feathered variety. Pigeons and that.
MARI: You what? Oh, frig me no . . .
Can't be doing with that.
All that cooing and flapping and shitting all over 'shop?
They want shooting, them.
The only good pigeons are in pies.
MARI *begins to lead them down the stairs.* GEORGE *smiles*
at BILLY *before they follow her.*

INT. LITTLE VOICE'S BEDROOM. DAY.
LV *listens on. The camera now closes in on her as she, strangely,*
breathes in sharply every time Judy does.

SOUNDTRACK: *High as a mountain, deep as a river,*
come rain or come shine
I'm gonna love you, I'm gonna love you,
I'm gonna love you . . .

INT. DOWNSTAIRS SHOP. DAY.

From the bottom of the stairs MARI *leads* GEORGE *and* BILLY
through the musty shell of an old shop that is their ground floor.
MARI *flicks the light switch but no light comes on. As they*
continue through, we see ancient dust-covered record players,
empty record racks, aged repair equipment etc. It is as if somebody
had a shop here once and died and nobody's touched it since.
They reach the front corner door.

GEORGE: Right, if you could just sign this, er . . . Mrs . . . ?
MARI: Hoff. Mari Hoff. Crappity name, in't it?
      Me late husband Frank left it me.
      You can imagine my feelings on signing marriage
      register: 'Mr and Mrs F. 'Off.'
      They laugh. BILLY *and* GEORGE *make to leave.*
MARI: Ta very much, Mr Cable.
GEORGE (*winks*): See you then.
BILLY (*quietly*): See you.
      She ignores him. After they walk out, MARI *closes the door*
      firmly with her bottom.

INT. LITTLE VOICE'S BEDROOM. DAY.
The noise of the front door snaps LV *out of her semi-trance. She*
goes to her window.

EXT. SHIPLEY STREET. DAY.
GEORGE *and* BILLY *climb into their van.*

GEORGE: What's it like then eh? To watch a Master at
        work?
        Did you not see her? Legs o' jelly she had for me.
        Husband dead and out of the way n'all, eh?
        BILLY *looks at his watch.*

10

GEORGE: Oh, bloody hell. Here's me imagining all sorts of
Slap 'n' Tickle, and all you can dream about is bloody
'Duane'.

BILLY *glances up at* LV*'s window. A blur as she dodges
away. But she was there. They get into the van.*

INT. KITCHEN. HOUSE. DAY.
In the background, LV *comes silently down the stairs and into the
front room, picking up the newspaper in the hall. In the kitchen,*
MARI *lights less than half a cigarette and searches the kitchen for
some food. She opens the fridge and recoils, closing it quickly.*

MARI: Hey, LV, we out of rashers? Recent rashers, I mean?
*She searches some more, and just for a moment her
shoulders drop. Just for this private micro-second, it seems,
she is tired of life. She picks herself back up to speed as she
returns to the front room. Passing the new phone on the
way:*
MARI: Oh, come on, phone, *ring.*

INT. FRONT ROOM. HOUSE. DAY.
MARI *flops on to the sofa.* LV *is sitting in another chair, reading
the newspaper, eating a Ryvita.*

MARI: Make us a cuppa, love, eh?
Look after me.
Ey, give us that paper.
LV *does.*
MARI: Oh, take it back, I don't like the front.
Oh, go on, eh, shove us some food on summat, LV,
go on.
Slap some food about for me, love. Go on.
Watches LV *munch on a Ryvita.*

11

What you eating anyway, a brown envelope?

What's on 'telly?

Turns it on . . . and off again before it even comes on.

Oh sod that.

Oh sod this.

I'm off down 'caff, me.

Can't start the day without some dribbling fat, can I?

Ey, speaking of which, I can call Sadie on me new instrument. That'll freak her flabby arse.

Goes into hall, picks up the phone, taps out a number.

Hey and listen you:

If anyone phones before I return . . .

this is more important than your life, girl . . .

Tell 'em I'll be back in five minutes.

All right?

All right??

ARE YOU RECEIVING ME?

LV *nods a tiny nod, before* MARI *gets through on the phone.*

MARI: Aye, Sadie, it's me . . . Aye, calling long distance.

Haar!

That I am, Sexy, well and truly plugged in.

Hey, listen. You, me, caff, now.

Last one out the door pays.

Right? OK, leg-over and out.

She hangs up, grabs a coat and makes for the door in an ungainly sprint.

Five minutes, tell 'em, right?

Toodle-pip.

EXT. SHIPLEY STREET. DAY.

MARI *bursts out of the door a fraction later than* SADIE, *her enormous neighbour across the street.*

MARI: Fuck me, mention a bacon butty and she shifts like
      Linford frigging Christie. How are you, Sexy?
SADIE: O-K.
MARI: You look a bit on peckish 'side to me.
      Move it!

INT. BT VAN. COASTAL ROAD. DAY.
BILLY *and* GEORGE *motor towards their next job.* GEORGE *is
on a rant.*

GEORGE: You stick with me, son, you'll learn a few tricks.
      'Reading matter', that's the best one.
      Next day or summat . . . when hubby's out, you go
      back . . . with 'Reading Matter'.
      Leaflets and that.
      Works every time.
      Bedtime reading I call it.
      He chuckles to himself. This stops when he sees BILLY
      looking up fretfully at the birdless skies.

INT. CAFÉ. DAY.
MARI *and* SADIE *march into the sleepy café. A few elderly out-
of-season trippers sit at tables with mugs of tea.*

MARI: Bangers and bubble and a fuck hot tea, ta. Twice.
      *Although the Café Royal this is not, the owner is still
      disappointed by such clientele.* MARI *and* SADIE *slide on
      to a table, still talking.*
MARI: Oooh, but Sadie, what a night I had me last night, eh?
      What a frigging championship night.
      You shoulda seen me.
      Queen for a night, I was.
      Never guess 'oo.

13

SADIE *looks blank*, MARI *pauses for effect.*
MARI: Ray Say.

FLASHBACK. INT/EXT. RAY'S CAR. SEAFRONT.
NIGHT.
*A bright red, gigantic Cadillac glides along the glitzy seafront,
humming with amusement arcades. North Yorkshire's flimsy
answer to Vegas glows on the promenade, reflected in the
windscreen, as the camera moves along the car to catch* RAY SAY
*in close-up. One hand on the wheel, the other draped over the side
of the car, he's all snakeskin loafers, Triumph belt buckle, cowboy
tie, slicked-back hair. Mutton dressed way too young. A fifty-
five-year-old face that looks like it's seen seventy-five of failure.*

MARI (*voice-over*): Ray frigging Say. You know him.
    Agent to the Stars. King of Cabaret. Manager of
    Miracles . . .
    Well, in this neck of the woods anyway.

FLASHBACK. EXT. MR BOO'S CLUB. NIGHT.
*We see his car pull up outside a large, tatty, quirky, weather-
beaten building on the seafront. A faulty neon sign flickers above
it: 'Mr Boo's'.*

MARI (*voice-over*): Up Mr Boo's nightclub all the time.
    Him that has that slight look of Elvis about him.
    You know him. Everyone knows him.
    And he knows everyone.

FLASHBACK. INT. BOO'S SHOW CLUB. NIGHT.
*A very spacious, sparsely populated but smoke-filled, sleazy
show club, the bottom rung of the entertainment ladder.* RAY

14

enters, a cross between Mafia and Royalty, nodding a hello to a bouncer and strutting confidently through towards the bar. He nods a hello across towards MR BOO, *a club owner through and through. He wears a crumpled well-worn tux that looks like it's never seen the light of day. The same goes for its occupant.* MR BOO *waves* RAY *over to join him and a small group that includes* MARI, *dressed to the nines. She stares across at* RAY.

MARI (*voice-over*): It were Mr Boo himself that introduced us, the other night . . .

FLASHBACK. INT. BOO'S SHOW CLUB. NIGHT.
Cut to later: The same gang laughing and drinking, RAY *by* MARI's *side, holding court with* BOO.

MARI (*voice-over*): And two seconds, Sadie, I fib you not, two seconds and his hand's on my arse.
My arse, my golden old arse in Ray Say's hand, while he stands there talking turns with Mr Boo.
We see said hand on said arse, as their owners give away nothing.

FLASHBACK. INT. BOO'S SHOW CLUB. NIGHT.
A different night. On the dance floor, RAY *manoeuvres* MARI *around like a butcher might a side of bacon and she dreamily enjoys every moment.*

MARI (*voice-over*): Saw him again up club last night.
The music was in our heads . . .
in our heads and in his wandering hands.
He's one of them . . . lovable twat sort of types . . .
Driving round in his lovable twatmobile . . .

15

FLASHBACK. INT/EXT. RAY'S CAR/STREETS. NIGHT.
Spectacular shots as RAY *takes* MARI *for a serious spin. The cold sea air rushing through her hair, coloured promenade lights flashing by, screeching round empty town at high speed,* MARI *shrieking.*

MARI (*voice-over*): Oh, he motored me round about a million
   miles an hour.
   Don't know what kind of car it is –
   one of them big wanky yank ones that just bloody *go*.
   Crack oh round 'bloody houses we was.
   Me heart in me mouth,
   his hand up me skirt,
   and me mind on his meat and veg.

FLASHBACK. EXT. HARBOUR JETTY. NIGHT.
The camera tracks slowly past three different cars each rocking in their own different way. This is Shaggers' Pier. The third car, creaking and grinding more grandly than the others, is RAY'S. *A number plate –* RAY.

MARI (*voice-over*): Then it's down to 'harbour for a pronto
   snog, lip-lapping like old hell.
   But at least he knows how to slide and dart and take a
   throat, and at least there's the thick wad of his wallet up
   against your tit for comfort . . .
   Up and down and down and up and under the bloody
   stars. Oooh . . . Heaven it were, Sadie.

INT. CAFÉ. DAY.
We snap out of the flashback on the stunned drop of a teaspoon. MARI *stops as she sees all the disapproving elderly eyes are on her.*

16

MARI: What's up wi' you lot? Never had a shag in a
Chevvie?
We hear the awful ringing of the tacky new phone . . .

INT. HALLWAY. HOUSE. DAY.
*LV is stranded in the hall, staring at the ringing phone. She looks
like a rabbit caught in the headlights. To double her worries, there
is suddenly a ding-dong doorbell from the front door downstairs.
Torn between two no-noes, she opts for the furthest. The door. She
exits downstairs.*

INT/EXT. DOWNSTAIRS SHOP. DAY.
She opens the front door an inch, to see BILLY.

BILLY (*shy*): Hiya . . . er, I forgot to leave you the 'reading
matter'.
About . . . services and all that.
She looks at the leaflet he's holding.
Yer phone's ringing.
She nods. He sees her discomfort.
Want me to get it for you?
She smiles gratefully, nods, and lets BILLY in.

INT. HALLWAY. HOUSE. DAY.
*LV leads BILLY up into the hallway, where he rushes to pick up
the phone, but picks it up too late.*

BILLY: Dead.
*There is a huge, seemingly interminable silence as the two of
them struggle for something to say. BILLY lets out a slight
noise, but to describe it as a word would be a colossal
flattery. Breaking this painful minute's silence, we hear*

17

footsteps on the stairs, the hall door opens and MARI *enters. Loud.*

MARI: Hey up, what's this then, eh? One of them 'rave' things?

(*Covers her ears sarcastically.*) Ooh, stop it, me ears won't take it!

Ey, I thought you were done, you.

You suddenly remember a socket you hadn't plugged? Eh? Telephone Bill? Little Birdy Boy?

BILLY: No, I just forgot to leave this . . . reading matter.

Tells you about servi . . .

MARI: Ey, did he call, LV? Did he ding-a-ling, eh?

Oh, for fuck's sake, *speak*, girl.

BILLY: We just . . . missed a call . . .

MARI *stops in her tracks, gapes at him.*

The gape turns to a glare, BILLY *quickly dials a number.*

BILLY: You can do 1471.

The glare is turning to a murderous one.

Tells you who was ringing.

It's one of the services . . . mentioned in . . . 'reading matter'.

Jots number down. There you go.

MARI (*reads it*): Doesn't say a name, then?

BILLY: No, no . . . afraid we're not quite that advanced yet.

He flashes a smile at LV *who smiles back, shyly. Tapping out the number,* MARI *sees this exchange.*

MARI: Aye, well, you'd best advance on out, eh?

Ta for everything but just . . . flap off, eh?

BILLY *shuffles out past* LV. *He tries to look her in the eye but she turns away. As the door closes, a strange sort of emptiness reappears in* LV*'s eyes. She slowly returns upstairs to her room as* MARI *speaks on the phone.*

MARI: Bloody hell I don't even know who I'm ringing here.

. . . Hello?

'Booze'? What?

Oh, Mr Boo's!

(*Sudden telephone voice*:) Hello, is Mr Say there presently please? Hit's Mari 'Hofe.

INT. BAR RENDEZ-BOO. DAY.

MR BOO *in the same old tux, hands over the phone to* RAY. *They are sitting on stools at the bar, behind which we see various Boo logos (Boo's Booze, Maliboo Cocktails, Booers' Droop etc.) On stage in the distance, across the empty room, a* STRIPPER *gyrates.*

RAY: Ray Say.

Oh, hello, love. Oh, just working, you know . . .

Giving Mr Boo here a shufty at me client list.

We getting it together later or what? Course I do, yeah.

See you up Red Lion then, yeah . . . OK, dove. See you.

MR BOO (*hangs up the phone for him*): You messing with that Mari Hoff?

RAY: Hoff and on.

MR BOO: More on than hoff, I imagine.

They chuckle. The music continues but the stripper has stopped gyrating.

STRIPPER: Ey, are you watchin' this or what?

RAY (*to* MR BOO): She'll go far, this one.

MR BOO: Aye, Scunthorpe if she's lucky.

RAY: Not interested? Good nipples.

MR BOO: Heating's off, that's why. Mine are the same.

RAY (*sighs, then shouts*): Thanks, love!

STRIPPER *sulkily picks up her kit and stomps off stage.*

RAY: You'll like this next lot, Mr Boo.

Singing combo, five lads, all built like Buddha . . .

MR BOO: What're they called?

19

RAY: 'Take Fat'.

> RAY *lights another nervous cigarette as some raunchy music starts up.* MR BOO*'s face gawps in horror at whatever's on the stage.* RAY *sees the gawp and fears he's in for another fruitless morning.*

EXT. PIGEON HILL. DAY. (DUSK)
It is late afternoon. BILLY, *sitting on his pigeon shack steps, scours the skies. A dog-walker,* ARTHUR, *passes.*

ARTHUR: Now then, Billy. Did he win then?
BILLY: Not come in yet, Arthur.
ARTHUR (*looks at his watch*): Not like your Duane.
> Don't worry, Billy lad, he'll be back before dark.
BILLY*'s POV of the bay dissolves into night. We hear the start of:*

> 'The Man That Got Away' *– by Judy Garland*

EXT. HOFF HOUSE. SHIPLEY STREET. NIGHT.
We see the coloured flicker of television through the drawn tatty curtains of the Hoff house, and hear the muffled music from A Star Is Born.

SOUNDTRACK: *The man that won you has run off and undone you*
> *That great beginning has seen a final inning*
> *Don't know what happened, it's all a crazy game . . .*

INT. FRONT ROOM. HOUSE. NIGHT.
Judy croons onstage while the camera finds and circles round LV,

*enthralled, watching the video on TV. She sits on the sofa, her
knees drawn up to her chin, her feet poking out of the bottom of a
dressing-gown. She looks like an owl. But a happy one. Her face
is lit up not just by the television but also by the content, she is
filled and thrilled with childish enjoyment . . . which flies out the
window with the opening of the door.* MARI *bursts in, flinging on
lights. Very drunk.*

MARI: Right you, you've got a fucking second to get in
shape.
She smacks the TV off and returns to the door.
Perk, girl, perk! Aye, come in, Ray, come in.
Here he is. Mr Ray Say.
She holds her hand out grandly towards the door and RAY
enters, unsteadily. LV *is paralysed with shyness.*
MARI: Here it is . . . Me home, me walls, me telly . . . my
phone, . . .
me daughter.
RAY (*very drunk also*): 'Ow do.
MARI: Ray.
Sun Ray, Sting Ray, Ray Gun, me very own Ronnie
Raygun!
Haar! Ooh I'm just frigging into him so.
She kisses him, long and hard. He kneads her golden arse.
(*Then, to* LV:) Well, say hello at least.
Oh, she's a misery, a miserable bloody misery.
What you having, Raymondo?
RAY: What you got?
MARI: Everything your throbbing throat could desire, lover
boy.
MARI *goes to the bar as* RAY *makes a poor show of hiding
his disinterest in* LV.
RAY: All right?
LV, *shocked, looks to the floor.* MARI *struggles back to the
top of the bar with a boxful of bottles – Malibu, Bailey's*

21

Irish Cream, crème de menthe etc.

MARI (*proudly*): Ta-daaa!

RAY: I'll have . . . a cup of tea.

MARI: You what?

> *He laughs, 'daaa!' – gotcha.*
> 'He'll have a cup of tea!'!! Haar!!
> LV, *suddenly embarrassed, heads out for the stairs.*

MARI: Hey, don't just go off like that, you . . . Hey!

RAY: Leave her, she's all right.

MARI: No, it's not all right, she spoils everything, her.
> I'm trying to make an impression here and
> she can't even be swivel to a friend, the tiny *little SLIT!!*
> *She kicks a tatty old pouffe across the floor, fiercely.*
> Oh, what am I doing and in front of you!
> Oh, well, that's it, I give up.
> This is me crappity home, and this is how I am, Ray.
> No gracey airs, and if you don't like it piss off out of it.

RAY (*stands*): Hey, hey, calm down. Don't get mad at *me.*
> I didn't say anything about anything.

MARI (*pause, what the hell*): OK, come on then, let's roll
> about. Haar!
> *She pulls him in a tango and throws him towards the sofa.*
> *The drink he's just poured goes flying. She jumps on. They*
> *laugh together, screaming, hooting, snogging and rolling*
> *about like kids.*

INT. LITTLE VOICE'S BEDROOM. NIGHT.

We hear MARI *laughing crudely downstairs, almost purposefully*
loud so LV *can hear.* LV *hurries to put on a record, relieved to*
lower the needle on to the record and drown out the noise below
with the bellowing opening of:

> *'That's Entertainment' – by Judy Garland*

INT. FRONT ROOM. HOUSE. NIGHT.
Infuriated, MARI *breaks off from* RAY.

MARI: Oh, here we go, on and on and frigging . . .
   Shut that racket, girl . . . !
RAY (*grabs her, calms her*): Hey, hey, calm down. She's all right.
MARI: Ooh, you . . . my little Ray-ver.
   She attacks him again. More lewd very loud laughter.
SOUNDTRACK: *The clown, with his pants falling down*
          Or the dance, that's a dream of romance
          Or the scene, where the villain is mean –
          That's entertainment . . .

INT. LITTLE VOICE'S BEDROOM. NIGHT.
As the noise of her mother's sordid fun gets louder, LV *turns up the volume even further on the record player. Even still, she covers her ears to blot out the laughter from downstairs. She looks across the room at the photo of her and her father.*

SOUNDTRACK: *The lights, on the lady in tights*
          Or the bride, with the guy on the side
          Or the ball, where she gives him her all –
          That's entertainment

INT. FRONT ROOM. HOUSE. NIGHT.
MARI *can't take the noise, even her own. She breaks from* RAY*'s passionate clinch and storms to the doorway.*

SOUNDTRACK: *The plot can be hot simply teeming with sex*
          A gay divorcee who is after her ex,
          it can be Oedipus Rex
          where a chap kills his father
          and causes a lot of bother . . . etc.

23

MARI: Oh I'm not having this . . . Can't bloody
concentrate . . .
(*Yells upstairs:*) CULL IT, WILL YOU!
THINK OF THE FUCKING NEIGHBOURS!!
No change.
Right, sod the bitch, we'll have our own on.
*She strides to her own record player, a seventies music
centre and, forcing yet another plug into the already
overloaded socket (adaptors plugged into adaptors), raids
the singles rack, digs any old one out, and slams it on,
whacks it up to volume eleven –*

'It's Not Unusual' – by Tom Jones

– crashes in. RAY *automatically springs up and starts
bopping with* MARI. *A huge sound, the two record players at
once, fighting against each other, louder and louder – 'That's
Not Unusual Entertainment' (but it is), until: BANG! The
electrics blow. The lights go. The two records slur to a halt.*
MARI: Haar! You've blown me fuse!
*In the dark, she pulls him back down on to the sofa. They
laugh and play again, roll on to the floor, clothes are
removed. As the loud dirty laughter subsides we again just
hear Judy Garland from upstairs. A different song. A
hushed reprise of the song on TV:*

'The Man That Got Away'

SOUNDTRACK: *The night is bitter, the stars have lost their
glitter*
The winds grow colder, suddenly you're older
And all because of the man that got away
MARI *is down to her bra,* RAY*'s shirt is unbuttoned as the
frolicking continues. But* RAY *suddenly freezes, pops his
head up into the darkness.*
RAY: Hey . . . hey, shh . . . what's . . . ?
She got her own radio up there then?
24

MARI: Eh? Oh, no, that's her. That's LV.

RAY: What? No.

MARI: Yeah.

RAY: No.

MARI: Yeah.

RAY: No.

MARI (*irritated*): Yesss.

> *The camera tracks into* RAY's *amazed face.*

LV (*off*): 'No more his eager call,

> the writing's on the wall
>
> The dreams you've dreamed have all gone astray . . .'

INT. LITTLE VOICE'S BEDROOM. NIGHT.

LV *stands still in the middle of the darkened room, lit only by the golden street light. She still stares across at the photograph of her father on the wall above her bed. The camera creeps up on her from behind, and circles round to her face, revealing a sad, singing face. Every note, every nuance is Judy Garland, but this is Little Voice. Big Voice now.*

LV: 'The man that won you has run off and undone you

> That great beginning has seen a final inning
>
> Don't know what happened, it's all a crazy game.
>
> No more that old time thrill
>
> For you've been through the mill
>
> And never a new love will be the same.'

INT. FRONT ROOM. HOUSE. NIGHT

RAY (*releases himself, gets up*): I don't *believe* it.

MARI: Look, Ray, she plays records all the time.

> Every God sented sec.
>
> They're stuck in her head and she can sing 'em and it

25

gets on my *wick*, end of story.

Now *roll*, will yer?

The voice is getting louder now, RAY *approaches the doorway.*

RAY: Sssh . . . I'm listening.

INT. LITTLE VOICE'S BEDROOM. NIGHT.

LV: 'Good riddance goodbye

Every trick of his, you're on to

But fools will be fools and where's he gone to?

The road gets rougher, it's lonelier and tougher.

With hope you burn up, tomorrow he might turn up.

There's just no let up, the livelong night and day.'

INT. HALLWAY. HOUSE. NIGHT.

We see RAY *standing by the door listening and looking upstairs. Behind him,* MARI *tries to focus from the sofa.*

MARI: Come on, lover, I'm mad for it here.

She sees he is entranced, her drunken shoulders drop.

Oh, sod it, I'm off then.

She puts her head down and immediately falls asleep.

RAY*'s eyes light up with opportunity as he gazes up towards* LV*'s bedroom.*

INT. LITTLE VOICE'S BEDROOM. NIGHT.

LV *is standing, looking at the photo. Her song finally drops to a peaceful hush:*

LV: Ever since the world began,

there's nothing sadder than . . .

26

A one man woman, looking for . . .
the man . . . that got . . . away.
Fade to black.

INT. PIGEON LOFT. PIGEON HILL. DAY
Fade up.

     BILLY, *wrapped up, sitting, asleep on the floor among silent quiet pigeons. A warble wakes him with a start. Once he remembers where he is, he does a quick look round to see that the open cage marked 'Duane' is still empty. He groans sadly.*

INT. HALLWAY. HOFF HOUSE. DAY.
LV *pads down the stairs bleary-eyed but carefully in the morning gloom. As she dozily crosses the hall for the kitchen suddenly a lamp goes on and Tom Jones blares up to speed.* LV, *after a moment's understandable terror, goes to the front room and switches him off. She then potters back through towards the kitchen. Slightly more awake now.*

INT. KITCHEN. DAY.
LV *wanders into the kitchen, fills the kettle, and again tentatively switches it on. This time, SMACK, a shock from the switch. She jumps back. Then, another shock – a voice:*

RAY: Normal service resumed, eh?
     RAY *is standing on a kitchen chair, pliers and half a coat-hanger in hand having carried out his own brand of electrical repair in the fuse box high in the corner. His hairy chest and shiny medallion peek out from under one of* MARI's *pink floral dressing-gowns. Quite a sight for this time in the morning.*

27

RAY (*refers to his head, then the coat-hanger*): Bit of grey
matter and a bit of grey matter, all it takes.
Bit of nouse, bit of coat-hanger, and bingo, let there be
light.
Climbs down with as much dignity as he can muster.
But you want to get this lot seen to, you know.
Could fetch the house down.
Hey, and so could you with what you did last night.
Bloody marvellous that. Who else do you do?
LV *starts to leave, but then:*
RAY: No, don't go, I'm just interested.
With being in show business myself you see.
Didn't yer mum tell you? . . . No? . . .
Oh, well, never mind. Here look . . .
She tenses up, but he manoeuvres her towards a chair.
Let's plonk you down here, love, like the twinkling star
you are, and let me rustle you up one of Ray Say's
famous Breakfassays. I do 'em all the time for me
artistes when we're on foreign engagements, y'know.
It's not all glamour in this game.
He opens the fridge and recoils.
Fuck me.

INT. MARI'S BEDROOM. DAY.
MARI *opens an eye and lets out a pathetic croak. She's wrecked.*

INT. KITCHEN. HOUSE. DAY.
RAY *is searching the kitchen cupboards for a feasible breakfast as*
LV *sits at the kitchen table. She watches him, nervously.*

RAY: No, bloody marvellous what you did last night
Marvellous up there in the dark.
Something I'll never forget, that.

He cracks an egg into a frying pan. The yolk is green.

Aw, for fff . . .

LV *can't hide a tiny smile.*

RAY *wipes his hands on the dressing-gown.*

RAY: Tell you what, what say you and me continue our little chat down the caff-caff?

LV *looks petrified at the thought.*

RAY: No?

Oh and look at me, all dressed up with nowhere to go.

Finally she smiles a little smile. So does he.

INT. BATHROOM. HOUSE. DAY.

MARI *is staring at herself in the mirror, long and hard. She shakes her head slowly, while trying not to disturb her brain. She sniffs her armpits. Not bad. She primps her hair to no major effect.*

INT. KITCHEN. HOUSE. DAY.

RAY *squeezes a teabag's last juices into a mug of hot water and takes it to the still wary* LV.

RAY: There you go love, best I can do.

'Une tasse de thé à la Ray'

He sits down opposite her. Opposite but close. There is a long, long silence before LV *plucks up courage. She opens her mouth.*

Yeah? Go on, love, fire away.

LV (*tries to speak*): In show business . . .

She stops. Long pause.

RAY: In show business, yeah . . . ?

LV: In show business . . .

D . . . d . . . did you ever meet . . .

RAY*'s face encourages her to continue.*

LV: Shirley Bassey?

RAY: Shirley!? Dear old Shirley! Shirley Shirley Shirley . . .
To be honest, love, as far as I remember,
I don't think our paths ever actually crossed.
Met Des O'Connor, though. And Charlie Williams.
Freddie Mr Parrot Face Davies?
She's unimpressed.
Suppose the biggest name I ever met was Monro.
LV (*sudden huge excitement*): Marilyn?!
RAY (*lets her down gently*): Matt.
You remember him? The singing bus conductor?
(*Spots her disappointment.*) You like Marilyn, yeah?
LV: Yeah.
RAY: Hey, you can't do her as well, can you?
After a pause, LV *shakes her head.*
Go on, I bet you can.
Shakes her head again.
Oh, well, there you go . . .
LV (*suddenly, as Marilyn*): 'I have this thing about saxophone
players . . . I don't what it is . . . my spine turns to
custard and I get goosepimply all over.'
RAY (*stunned*): Frig me . . . that's amazing . . . !
Christ, I can't believe that!
Bloo-dee hell! Go on, who else do you do?
LV *shrinks, looks uncomfortable once again.*
RAY *moves in closer.*
RAY: Listen, LV, listen, you are my discovery.
I found you, right?
Me.
Always remember that.
In fact, here, have one of my new cards.
Reaches for tacky gold business card.
I left one out for you in case I missed you.
It's gold, look.
She is fascinated by the glint of it, but won't take it.
I wouldn't give one of these to just anyone, you know?
30

After an age, she finally takes it.
Now look, I know you're a bit on the quiet side, but I'm a big noise in these parts, you know, and together, you and me, we can set this place on fire.
You're a star, you!
He kisses her on the forehead, hard, then leaves. After he's gone:

LV: And you're a nutter.

INT. HALLWAY. HOUSE. DAY.
RAY *is dressing while he talks on the tacky new phone.*

RAY: I need to speak to him, now.
No, it can't wait, no.
Hold him there, I'm coming down now.
MARI *comes through the hallway as* RAY *finishes dressing. She looks a dreadful sight.*

RAY (*hides his initial shock*): Mari! You look . . . er . . .

MARI: No . . . don't speak . . . just . . . don't . . . speak for a minute . . .

RAY: I've got to go, Mari, but what can I say?
It's happened at last, eh!? It's like at the races when you know you're on to a certainty and you're feeling 'This is it! She is the one!!'
He gives her a huge kiss on his way out, then he's off down the stairs. It is a second before MARI *realises these are the nicest things anyone's ever said to her.*

MARI (*to herself*): I am . . . the . . . one?
She chases out after him.

EXT. HOFF HOUSE. SHIPLEY STREET. DAY.
RAY *is hopping into his car.* MARI *runs out and grabs him.*

31

MARI: Oh give us another one, Ray.

> *She smothers him in a kiss. It's virtually rape.*

RAY: Honest, Mari, I can't believe it!

> It's what I've been looking for, for ages.
>
> It's just . . . one of them once-in-a-lifetime things, eh?
>
> I've never felt like this before, about *anyone*.
>
> See you at the Seabirds later, eh . . . ?
>
> Thanks, Mari, that's all I can say . . . *Thank you!*
>
> SADIE *hears the commotion as she comes out of her house opposite. She crosses the road to join* MARI *as the Cadillac roars off leaving her gobsmacked in its slipstream.*

MARI: Bloody hell, Sadie. He wants me.

> The bastard wants me! Bugger me.
>
> SADIE *watches the car go, looks at* MARI, *sees her joy, does a strange enquiring little shuffle/dance.*

MARI (*points* SADIE *inside*): Too bloody right, Sade!

> Get up there and get it on. Our *fave bloody rave!*

INT. FRONT ROOM. HOUSE. DAY.

SADIE *runs to the old stereo and digs out a single and slams it on the record deck. Music crashes in:*

> 'Disco Inferno'

MARI (*yells*): At last! Saved! Secured!

> I shall go to the ball, oh you darlings from the sky!
>
> *They start to dance.* MARI *is a good dancer and gets into the groove.* SADIE *raunches, quite out of character with what we know about her so far. Jumps on the sofa, does a series of Michael Jackson pelvic thrusts, bounces off walls. The whole thing is a celebration. Joyous.* LV, *in the background, escapes from the kitchen, from the noise, and runs upstairs.*

MARI (*whoops*): Oh, what a life life can be!

32

INT. LITTLE VOICE'S BEDROOM. DAY.

LV *throws herself on to her bed and covers her head with her pillows. This kind of music is not to her liking.*

INT. FRONT ROOM. HOUSE. DAY.

SADIE, *standing on the sofa, topples over with it and crashes to the floor. They are both screaming with laughter. We can just hear a doorbell ringing.*

INT/EXT. DOWNSTAIRS SHOP. DAY.

MARI *opens the front door just as* GEORGE *is about to finally knock on it.*

MARI: Oh, bloody hell, what now?

GEORGE: Eh? . . . er, forgot to leave you this.
Reading Matter.

MARI: I only ordered a phone, not a mobile bloody library.

GEORGE: What?

MARI: Young birdy boy's already been and done all that.
Come on, off out of it, make way for a Woman in Lust.
MARI *and* SADIE *clump out past the drop-jawed* GEORGE, *slamming the door behind them.* GEORGE *thinks . . .*

EXT. PIGEON HILL. DAY.

BILLY *tips feed into his loft, the pigeons go crazy for it. He sees* GEORGE *marching up the hill. He shouts from a distance.*

GEORGE: Hey! You, you twat! What you think you're bloody playing at?!

BILLY: Feeding.

GEORGE (*arrives*): Feeding my arse, screwing around more

33

like! You come on all quiet like you're only interested in these bloody things here, but really you're a devious little bastard aren't you, eh?

BILLY *looks understandably confused.*

GEORGE: You know what I'm on about – 'Reading Matter.'
A penny drops.

Ah, yes, you little bastard, though what you want to get your leg over that for I'll never know.

Old enough to be your bloody grandma.

BILLY (*how could he think such a thought?*): I went to see the girl, George, the one with the music.

GEORGE: What . . . her upstai . . . ? Oh, Jesus, I thought . . .

BILLY: Just . . . to . . . talk to her, like.

GEORGE (*nudge nudge*): Oh aye?

BILLY: Yeah. Thought she was . . . interesting.

GEORGE: Interesting like off her bloody rocker, you mean.

INT. NORTH SEA FISHERIES. DAY.
The frame is poured full of slimy fish, which are then covered white with ice. A wide shot reveals the harbourside fish market in action. Crates of fish being tipped out, weighed etc. A wet floor reflects the harbour. Among the activity we see SADIE *shovelling ice and* MARI *spraying water with a hose. She shouts above the noise.*

MARI: Didn't I say to you though, Sade, eh?!

I knew there was summat down for us, me and red-hot Ray?!

I just had that feeling in me twat-bone!

Ey, and you know me, I can predict rain with that!
They screech with laughter.

EXT. PIER. DAY.

MARI *and* SADIE *march quickly away from work.* MARI *faster than usual.*

MARI: I'm wearing me Share Price knickers tonight, me . . .
  Down as likely as up.
  And some shit-tight bloody bra.
  Cos I'm one high razzamatazz in here today, me!
  (Thumps her chest, shouts publicly across harbour:) It's like
  there's a circus parade passing over me paps!

EXT. SHIPLEY STREET. NIGHT
Close-up of BILLY, *who seems to hear the echo of* MARI *across town. But it is night now. He looks up towards the skies. Behind him, just for a second, the background seems to fall away magically, as if he is floating on the music which we begin to hear . . .*

  'My Heart Belongs To Daddy' – by Marilyn Monroe

SOUNDTRACK: *While tearing off a game of golf,*
      I may make a play for the caddie
      But when I do I don't follow through,
      Cos my heart belongs to daddy
      If I invite some boy, some night,
      to dine on my fine Fin and Haddie
      I just adore his asking for more but . . .
      my heart belongs to daddy . . .

INT. LITTLE VOICE'S BEDROOM. NIGHT.
As Marilyn continues on the turntable, LV *is dutifully cleaning and tidying her record collection. Behind her, we see a shape appear at the window. It is* BILLY, *looking like he is strangely just floating there.* LV *senses something behind her, turns, sees,*

35

and screams. A flying BT *man. He shouts through the closed window:*

BILLY: Just seeing if the wires are all right!
   Just seeing if the wires are all right!!
   JUST SEEING . . .
   She goes and opens the window.
   . . . if the wires are all right.
   A wide shot reveals that he is in fact on the van's extended crane platform, having whirred his way up to LV*'s top-floor window.*

INT. MARI'S BEDROOM. NIGHT.
MARI, *dolling herself up for a night out, thinks she hears something, but then shrugs it off.*

INT/EXT. LV'S BEDROOM. NIGHT
The very shy BILLY *starts to whistle as* LV *stares at him. He looks up and down the wall.*

BILLY: You go out much?
LV: No.
BILLY (*whistles again, then*): You a telly fan?
LV: No.
BILLY (*whistles again, manoeuvres platform*): Going anywhere
   for your holidays?
LV: No.
BILLY (*whistling trails off*): There are no wires.
LV: Eh?
BILLY: I finished work hours ago.
   Uh . . . I don't know what to say now.
   Another pause, they look at each other.
   I'm Billy. Can I ask your name?
36

LV: LV.

BILLY: Oh. Does that stand for something?

LV: Little Voice.

BILLY: Right, on account of being soft-spoken, like?

LV *nods*.

SOUNDTRACK: *Yes my heart belongs to daddy,*
so I simply couldn't be bad
Yes my heart belongs to daddy,
da da da da da da da da dad
So I want to warn you laddie,
though I think you're perfectly swell
But my heart belongs to daddy,
'cos my daddy he treats it so well . . .

BILLY: Nice tune, that.

LV: 'My Heart Belongs To Daddy'.

BILLY: Oh, . . . right.

LV: Marilyn Monroe.

BILLY: Oh, yeah, right.

Ey, your mam's a live wire, in't she? Bloody hell.

Not fond of pigeons, neither, is she?

LV: Pigeons?

BILLY: Aye. I keep 'em, you know. Homing pigeons.

I love 'em.

I'm up pigeon hill all the time, where lofts are.

Feed and exercise twice a day.

LV: Exercise?

BILLY: Aye, you let them out and they fly back.

That's what homing pigeons do.

Except for Duane, like.

LV: Duane?

BILLY: Me best bird. Not come back from France yet.

LV: What's he doing in France?

BILLY (*after a long confused pause*): Coming back here.

LV: Oh.

Another pause.

BILLY: Any road, it can be boring to the non-enthusiast.

LV: No, you're all right.

BILLY: When you let 'em go, see 'em fly, and better still see
'em back, it's like . . . dead exciting.

You'll have to come up there with me sometime, LV,
and see for yourself.

LV: I don't go out.

BILLY (*looks at her, disbelievingly*): What . . . never?

LV hears MARI's *stilettos clacking up her stairs. She
hurries to close the window, flapping for* BILLY *to go.*

LV: Best go, Billy, bye.

BILLY (*from behind glass*): See you again somewhere then,
eh?

*LV urges him to disappear. He drops obediently below the
window frame just as* MARI *enters, dressed to kill as
promised.* LV *acts casual.*

MARI: You talking to yourself n'all, now?

LV: No?

MARI: Aye, well, I'm off out on the razz now.

You have a nice night in with yer pals, eh?

LV looks at her LPs, nods, and MARI *exits with a
look of disdain.* LV *goes to the window but* BILLY *has
gone.*

EXT. SEABIRDS PUB. NIGHT.
An excited MARI *trots up the steep hill to the pub. She has tried
hard, frockwise. All brash sparkle like her attitude. But very
short. She continually has to tug down her rear hem in order to
maintain some semblance of decency . . .*

INT. BACK BAR. SEABIRDS PUB. NIGHT.
. . . and struts into the pub. She spots RAY *and* MR BOO *at the
far end of the bar. She hides her disappointment in* BOO's

38

presence and waves playfully to RAY *who beckons her over,*
eagerly.

RAY: Bloody hell, where've you been? I said eight.
MARI: Aye, but look at me, lover, eh?
Takes time to get up like this.
Arndale Centre weren't built in a day, you know.
RAY: Aye, and with half as much plaster.
MARI: *Haar!* You smooth talker, you!
RAY: Yeah, right, well . . . You know Mr Boo from 'club,
yeah? Little Voice's mum.
MARI *seems confused by the mention of her daughter.*
MR BOO: Aye. Once-in-a-lifetime thing, Ray tells me.
Never felt like this before about anyone, he says.
MARI *stares at* RAY. *The wave she has been riding on all
day hits the shore. Hard.*
RAY: So. We'll get a few quick drinks down us, eh?
And then it's back to yours so we can have a listen.
A spot of 'Who Do You Do?' for Mr Boo, like.
MARI *is stunned.*
MR BOO: What you having, love?
MARI: Gin.
Double.
And a Campari chaser.
She stares at RAY, *who smiles back.*

EXT. SEABIRDS. NIGHT.
MARI, *drunk, wobbly, deflated, follows* RAY *and* BOO *down the
hill towards* RAY's *car.*

MARI: Oh, God, you make me sick, you lot.
First that little phone fart and now you.
All drooling over that little stick o' shite.
I've got tits n'all, you know?

And a gob on me for every occasion.

Tits, gob, and an arse to die for, me!!

RAY: (*opens car door, proudly*): Good-looker, eh, Boo?

MR BOO: Just as well, with that mouth.

RAY: The car, Boo. The car.

MR BOO: Oh. Aye. Yeah, very nice.

INT. LITTLE VOICE'S BEDROOM. NIGHT.

LV *is sitting in her nightie with album covers surrounding her on the floor. Her light's on. It's warm, cosy. She listens adoringly to a chirpy record:*

'The Dicky Bird Hop' – by Gracie Fields

SOUNDTRACK: *Ooo-h the chirruping of the birdies on the sycamore tree*
They're lucky to be so happy and free
I know that they're chirruping out a little rhythm to me
I hear them saying early every morn:
Geddup, geddup, geddup . . .

MARI (*crashes in*): *Geddup*, you, Ray wants you. Downstairs.

LV: What for?

MARI: (*grumpily*): You know what for.

You've got him thinking you can do summat or summat.

Wants you down anyway.

Show Mr Boo what you can doo.

LV: It's private.

MARI: Private, my privates. You're just damn selfish and useless, you, and you can do nought but whisper and whine like your father before you. Couple of bloody nothings, the pair of you.

LV *hides behind an LP cover.*

40

MARI *looks around the room.*

MARI: Look at it . . . racks and racks of dirty old discs and a clapped-out player.

The sum of your father's life.

Just a pile of old junk no fucker wants.

Now come on! Downstairs.

She snatches the cover from LV, *who snatches it back, surprisingly violently.*

LV (*growls*): Don't you dare touch these, *ever!*

MARI *looks at her with fury. She kicks the record player, silencing the song, and leaves, switching the main light off and slamming the door on the way. As she goes, she snarls:*

MARI: Up yours, stick-leg!

Street light still catches LV*'s face as she stares across at the picture of her father which is still but barely lit by a tiny golden light above, the solitary glimmer in the dark. She walks towards it.*

MARI (*off*): She'll not come down.

RAY (*off*): What?

MARI (*off*): Just like I said, she'll not sing, I told you.

MR BOO (*off, brassed off*): What's happening, Say?

LV *kneels on her bed and looks up to the picture. A tiny whispered cry in the near dark:*

LV: Dad. Dad. Dad. Dad. Dad. Dad. Dad . . .

INT. HALLWAY. HOUSE. NIGHT.

MR BOO *walks to the door, shaking his head, his time wasted once more.*

MR BOO: Well, I'm sorry, Ray, but Boo's a busy man.

I've got to be off. Got other acts to see.

Acts that can be bothered. Night all.

RAY *and* MARI *follow him down the stairs.*

EXT. SHIPLEY STREET. NIGHT.
MR BOO *and* RAY *come out of the house,* RAY *trying to bar* MR
BOO*'s way.* MARI *stays standing in the doorway.*

RAY: No, hold on, Boo, it won't take a minute . . .
    Honest, believe me, she's dead special.
    With that MARI *groans, turns and goes back into the*
    house.
MR BOO: Listen, Say, I didn't get where I am today by
    wasting me time listening to singers that don't sing.
    All I can say is she stands an outside chance as a mime
    act.

INT. DOWNSTAIRS SHOP. NIGHT.
MARI *walks back through the shop. As she passes it, she kicks*
dad's old office chair over with meaningful venom.

INT. LITTLE VOICE'S BEDROOM. NIGHT.
A crack of light appears on LV*'s wall and bed, as if the door has*
opened slightly. She opens her eyes. In the crack of light, a large
shadow looms. LV *puts her hand gently on the shadow and*
whispers:

LV: Dad . . .
    She turns to look towards the door. We see in the golden
    light of the doorway the black and white image of her
    father, the MAN*, dressed and looking as if he has*
    stepped straight out of the photograph. LV *smiles*
    warmly.

INT. HALLWAY. HOUSE. NIGHT.
MARI *comes in through the door angrily and marches towards*

42

the front room. She stops suddenly, freezes, as she hears the tiniest sound from further upstairs.

'Over The Rainbow'

LV (*offscreen; a prefect imitation of Judy Garland*):
'Somewhere over the rainbow, way up high
There's a land that I heard of once in a lullaby . . .'
MARI *races back to the door and downstairs.*

EXT. SHIPLEY STREET. NIGHT.
MR BOO *is on his way up the street.* RAY *shouts after him.*

RAY: Look, you know me, Boo, I wouldn't fetch you down
here for nothing. You've got to . . . hear . . .
Suddenly LV *gets hugely loud, her voice cutting through the night air and down to the street from her window high above.*
LV (*offscreen*): 'Somewhere over the rainbow . . .'
BOO *stops, turns and listens.*
MARI *rushes out of the door but sees they've already noticed.*
Amazed, BOO *slowly returns to* RAY*'s side below* LV*'s window.)*
LV (*offscreen*): 'Skies are blue,
And the dreams that you dared to dream
really do come true.'

INT. LITTLE VOICE'S BEDROOM. NIGHT.
A voice so loud you couldn't believe it came from such a tiny girl. A perfect impression. The camera wraps round LV *and her father.*

LV: 'Some day I'll wish upon a star
and wake up where the clouds are far behind me . . .'

43

As the song continues, the camera glides down towards the
stunned faces of RAY *and* MR BOO *as they gape up in awe at the*
dark window. MARI *watches them.*

LV (*offscreen*): 'Where troubles melt like lemon drops
away above the chimney tops
That's where you'll find me.'

MR BOO (*finally voicing his disbelief*): That's never her!

RAY: It is.

MR BOO: No.

RAY: Yeah.

MR BOO: No.

RAY: Ye-ah.

MR BOO (*pause*): No.

MARI: Oh here we go again!

MR BOO (*excited*): That's *Judy!* You've got Judy Garland in
there.

MARI: Oh aye, she's round here all the time.
Her and that Shirley Bassey, drinking our bloody cocoa.

MR BOO: You have a remarkable daughter there, Mrs Hoff.

MARI: Oh, don't I bloody know.

MR BOO: Well, Ray, we must have her if you can arrange it.
There's the makings of a first-class act there, real class.
We could do a lot with that.

RAY (*sees his chance*): Right, Mari, love, Boo and me's off up
the pub.
Talk finer details and finances. Leave the latch off,
eh?

MARI (*grabs his arm as he moves to go*): Ey, what about me
then? Where do I fit in, eh?
Me, the fucking *second-class act?*

RAY (*sensing trouble*): Er, mine's a double Scotch, Boo, see
you up there, eh?

MR BOO *makes his way up the street.*

44

RAY (*while above them the song continues*): What are you
   saying, Mari?
   I'm telling you, love, you're sitting on a gold mine.
   Never mind 'Over The bloody Rainbow', up there in
   that bloody bedroom.
   'Dreams that you dare to dream . . .', eh?
   She can make them come true.

INT. LITTLE VOICE'S BEDROOM. NIGHT.
LV *has sat up in bed singing directly to her black and white
father. As she sings about bluebirds, they both do an action from
the past, a little flutter of their hands. They smile at each other at
the memory.* LV*'s smile is tainted by a tear.*

EXT. SHIPLEY STREET. NIGHT.

RAY: She's our chance, Mari.
   We've been shovelling shit long enough, you and me.
   Now's our chance to step out of it.
MARI: *Our* chance?
RAY (*smiles assuringly*): I'm going nowhere without you, girl.
   MARI *stares at him a second, unsure, then, back to the
   overconfident* MARI *we know, she lunges in . . .*
MARI: Ooh, Elvis breath! (*They kiss.*)
   Come on, then. Lead us to the dotted line!
   *They chuckle their way excitedly up the street as the camera
   climbs slowly through the blue of night up to* LV*'s bedroom.
   Music plays under her now as she reaches the climax of her
   song:*
LV (*offscreen*): 'Somewhere over the rainbow, bluebirds fly
   Birds fly over the rainbow,
   why oh why can't I?'

45

INT. LITTLE VOICE'S BEDROOM. NIGHT.
From her bed, LV *still stares, still sings, possessed.*

LV: 'If happy little blue birds fly . . .
beyond the rainbow . . .
Why then oh why can't I?'
The MAN *smiles a goodnight smile and closes the door. We
see the shaft of light narrow on the sad goodbye in her eyes
as the door closes. In the complete darkness now, she rolls
over and settles down to sleep.*
Fade to black.

INT. LITTLE VOICE'S BEDROOM. NIGHT.
*After a couple of seconds of black, we hear thuds, whispers and
giggles. Then a bang of a door and a flick of a switch. Bright light
that wakes* LV. *She springs up in shock and sees, standing
unsteadily at the door her father seems to have just closed,* MARI
and RAY, *both even more drunk than before. They stagger
towards her bed.*

LV: Wha . . . ? . . . uh . . .
MARI: Love, lovey, don't worry, it's only us. Me and Ray.
Coming bearing good news, milady.
RAY: Stupendoussnews ashually.
MARI: Mr Boo would like you to sing at his club . . . On
stage.
RAY: Sing what you like.
LV (*shakes her head*): No. Nnnn.
MARI: No, listen, love. He'll pay. Good money, n'all.
Could be up to fifty quid, right, Ray?
RAY: Right, and that's just the start of it.
LV: No.
MARI: Ray'll look after you, he knows all about showbiz.
And all you have to do is sing.

46

Sing, like what you do best anyways.

You might feel shy, I know like what you are . . .

RAY: Nothing wrong with being shy, at first.

MARI: Natural, that.

LV *has squeezed herself tight in the corner of the room by her pillow. She pulls the bedclothes around her.*

RAY: Had a girl recently wouldn't say boo to a goose.

Now she's topping the bill at the Reform Club.

MARI: Who's that? That stripper?

RAY: Well, yes, but it's similar, isn't it, similar case, Tina.

LV (*whispers*): Please go. Please . . .

MARI: Besides which, it'll get you out, LV love.

Not healthy being cooped up in here like a . . .

LV (*a gigantic roar*): JUST GO!!

RAY: Bloo-dy 'ell . . . that's gratitude for you.

Surprised, RAY *turns and leaves.* MARI *is in a state of embarrassment and sudden rage. She reaches the door, slams off the light, and viciously turns back in the dark and screams at* LV:

MARI: You . . . great long STREAK OF PISS!!

YOU ARE BLOODY DOING IT GIRL!!

Cut to black.

We hear the exciting drum of 'Showtime' and hear the substandard intro of MR BOO.

INT. STAGE. BOO'S CLUB. NIGHT.

MR BOO *is dressed to entertain, but sadly not trained to do so. His seedy face forces a smile of welcome to a handful of punters.*

MR BOO: Oh, come on, you can do better than that.

So, how are you all doing, alreet?

Muted response.

INT. BACKSTAGE. BOO'S CLUB. NIGHT.

LV, *pale and dressed in her ordinary everyday clothes, is being led somewhat forcefully down a dimly lit corridor in the bowels of* MR BOO'*s club by* RAY *and* MARI.

MR BOO: . . . so the manager says:
>'Would you like the condom on your bill, sir?'
>and the duck says:
>'Certainly not, what sort of duck do you think I am?'
>Now then, a true story this . . .

RAY: You're all right, LV.
>All you have to do is stand there and sing.
>Just like at home.
>Just stay calm and relaxed.
>LV *is shivering with tension.*

MARI: What are you on about relaxed? Look at her!

RAY: Think about Judy . . . Think about Shirley . . .
>Think about . . . *Marilyn.*
>*With that, he pushes her on to the stage where she finds herself behind the closed curtain and, even more frightening, behind a massive microphone. Through the curtain we can just see* MR BOO *trying to entertain the natives.*

INT. MR BOO'S CLUB. NIGHT.

We see the sparse club audience, a motley collection of middle-aged and older folk round several tables. Among them is SADIE. MARI *staggers over to join her at her table.*

MR BOO: Now then, as you know, Boo braves anything,
>goes anywhere, in his perpetual quest for fresh talent to
>spice up your midweek merriment here.
>*Behind the curtain,* LV *still gawps at the microphone.*
>But for all that, guess which exotic part of the world I
>found tonight's star turn?

48

Shipley Street . . .

Well, it saves on travel expenses, dun't it?

GEORGE, *drinking at the bar, is suddenly interested.* BOO
glances to the wings where RAY *gives him a thumbs-up.*

MR BOO: So anyway, pretty people, enough of me . . .

Cheers of agreement.

A talent, an undiscovered treasure, an act of wonder,
ladies and gentlemen, a little girl that's big, a northern
light, a rising star, order and hush, hush and order, for
the turn of turns, the one, the only . . . LITTLE
VOICE, ladies and gentlemen,

LITTLE VOICE!

MR BOO *stretches out an introductory arm as he leaves the
stage.* MARI *and* SADIE *both clap overenthusiastically.
The curtain rises.* LV *stands there. Still, except for a slight
tremble. She shields her eyes from the harsh spotlight. At the
bar,* GEORGE *stares agog.* RAY, *worried in the wings,
urges her on.*

RAY: Go on, love. *Go on!* You're on!

SADIE *has her heart in her mouth while the rest of the
audience shuffle their discomfort. Next to her,* MARI *spurts
a whispered stream, nay, torrent, under her breath:*

MARI: Go on go on sing,
I'll do anything just sing sing for fuck's sake sing.
CU on LV. *We see her POV, the sea of faces, the bright
blinding light. The silence is deafening. Finally, she opens
her mouth to sing, but nothing comes out. More unease
everywhere. A groan somewhere.* RAY *suddenly realises.*

RAY: The lights! It's the lights! Turn out the lights!

MR BOO *rolls his eyes in disbelief and pulls a switch. The
whole place is plunged into darkness. Surprise from the
audience, then silence again. A beer glass breaks. Finally,
and suddenly, in the silent darkness,* LV *starts to sing. You
can just make out her form huddled over the mike. Behind*

49

her, forming her shape, are tacky twinkly stars on the
backdrop. Eerie, and haunting in the dark, she sings a
hesitant but perfect impersonation of Billie Holiday:

'Lover Man'

LV: 'I don't know why, but I'm feeling so sad
   I long to try something I've never had.
   Never had no kissing, oh what I've been missing . . .'
   We see her eyes in the darkness, frightened, fretful, as they
   scan the audience, searching madly. But that's it. LV *stops*
   as suddenly as she started, eyes closed tight now. RAY
   whispers from the wings:

RAY: Do another one . . . go on! Do some more!
   LV *snaps into Judy Garland, speaking as she does in her*
   intro at Carnegie Hall.

   'Chicago'

LV: 'More? Do you really want more? Aren't you tired?
   Well, we only got one more, we'll do-we'll do-we'll do
   Chicago
   Chicago Chicago that toddling town
   Chicago Chicago I'll show you around
   I love it, bet your bottom dollar you'll lose the blues
   In Chicago, Chicago,
   The town that Billy Sunday could not shut down . . .
   On . . .'
   Again, a jolting halt as she dries. A whispered yell from
   RAY.

RAY: What you stopped for?
   Don't stop now . . . do anything.. Anything!
   And Jesus . . . look happy!
   We hear Marilyn Monroe.

   'Happy Birthday'

LV: Happy? . . . birthday to you
50

Happy birthday to you
Happy birthday Mr President
Happy birthday . . . to-o yo-ou.

The audience gets restless because they can't see. Another broken glass. There is the odd scoffing laugh and shout for light from the deep black of the audience. MR BOO *and* RAY *are in the wings, concerned.*

MR BOO: This is crazy, Ray. . . the punters can't see.

RAY (*reluctant*) All right, get them back up, get the lights back up!

MR BOO *throws the lights back up. The spot whacks down on* LV. *She opens her eyes. Again a rabbit caught in the headlights. She turns and runs offstage. In the wings,* LV *approaches* RAY *with her arms out. He holds his out, but she veers away from him, passes him and disappears down into the dark corridor still looking for somebody to hold. The audience are still frozen in their poses, mouths open. We expect abuse, but the impersonations were so stunning they don't know how to react. There is silence.* SADIE *is smiling proudly. She claps, not many follow suit.* MARI *has her head in her hands.* GEORGE *shakes his head sadly. In the wings* MR BOO *prepares to go onstage.*

MR BOO: Well, I thought it couldn't *go* downhill with you, Ray . . . What am I going to tell 'em?

RAY (*strangely elated*): Tell 'em . . . she'll be back.

INT/EXT. RAY'S CAR. SEAFRONT. NIGHT.

RAY *drives them all away from the club.* MARI *in the passenger seat,* SADIE *comforting the shell-shocked* LV *in the back.* MARI *is storming mad.*

MARI: Embarrassing! One hundred bloody chunk embarrassing, that.

I'm shown up. Which is more than she bloody was, stood there in 'bloody dark.

LV: He wasn't there.

MARI (*doesn't even hear, let alone listen*): And what was she singing? What the 'ell was THAT?

She could have made an effort and done some bloody Spice Girls or summat for Christ's sake, oh, I told you you was wasting your time on the little slit, she did the whole thing to spite mother. I know her. Oh go on, drop her off, dump her home and let's go eat.

LV *remains dazed, expressionless.*

EXT. PIGEON HILL. NIGHT.

BILLY *still waits for Duane. It is quiet and peaceful up here. He is shocked by a voice out of the dark.*

GEORGE: Now then.

BILLY: Jesus!

GEORGE: Guess what? I've just seen your bird.

BILLY: Where?

GEORGE: Onstage, down at Boo's.

BILLY (*seriously confused*) What?

GEORGE (*a long pause before he realises why*): Oh . . . no . . . not Duane . . . I mean the other one. That lass.

BILLY *still can't quite take it in.*

INT. HALLWAY. HOUSE. NIGHT.

The horrible ring of the horrible phone. LV *is staring at it. Finally she dares to answer it.*

LV (*tiny*): Hello?

BILLY (*off*): LV? You're in, then.

LV: Oh, hello . . .

EXT. TELEGRAPH POLE. PIGEON HILL. NIGHT.

BILLY *has a work-phone wired up to the spaghetti on a telegraph pole.*

    Cut between this and previous.

BILLY: Hey, listen, I've just heard about what you did
      tonight . . . at Boo's club . . .

LV: They made me.

BILLY: Who made you?

LV: 'im and 'er. They go on till you do.

BILLY: They trying to make you do it again?

LV: Don't think she liked it. Won't be doing it no more.

INT/EXT. 'JUST FOR THE HALIBUT' CHIPPIE. NIGHT.

*The Twatmobile is parked directly outside the warm bright glow
of an overcrowded steamy chippie. Inside,* RAY, MARI *and*
SADIE *queue for chips.*

MARI: Oh but, Ray, it were crap awful, weren't it?

RAY: Well, she's not what you'd call a performer, I grant you
      that, no, but I can take care of that.
      She just needs a big band or something to boost her
      confidence, big flashy stage set, bright lights, bit of glitz,
      snazzy frocks, all that.

MARI: Ooh, I love it when you talk swanky.

INT. HALLWAY. HOUSE. NIGHT.

LV *(smiles)*: Has Duane come home?

BILLY: No, not yet.
      Happens sometimes.
      They go for it, some of 'em.
      Once they're out, flying free . . . they like it.

53

(*Thinks about it, tries it:*) You should try it sometime,
LV.

LV (*hears the sound of the door downstairs*): I've got to go, I've
got to go . . .
She hangs up and runs upstairs.

EXT. TELEGRAPH POLE. PIGEON HILL. NIGHT.

BILLY: LV? . . .
He hangs up, disappointed.
(*Then, out of the blue:*) What was she like?
It is only now that we realise GEORGE *has also been
hanging at the top of the telegraph pole, helping on the
technical side. He heaves a tired sigh.*

GEORGE: Well . . . if it's a roller-coaster of unbridled
excitement you're after . . . Reckon you're better off
here.

INT. LITTLE VOICE'S BEDROOM. NIGHT.
LV *pretends to be asleep in her bed. The crack of light from the
door once more appears on her face. Again, the shadow of the*
MAN *is cast on her face and on the wall behind her. The light is
switched on.* RAY *stands there, clutching the sheet of paper.*

RAY: You're all right, love. Only me.
LV *is frightened, suspicious.*

RAY: Been working on the act. Planning and that.
Talked Boo into giving us another go and I got it all
worked out.
You'll love it.
Everything tailored to your personality.
All you have to do is step on from the side.
LV *shakes her head in fear.*

54

RAY: What's up?

Hey, angel, don't let a little hiccup like tonight put you off.

Happens to the best of them, that.

Points at the albums on the floor.

If you could ask her, or her, or her, they'd tell you the same.

They've *all* had nights like that, you know?

Haven't you, Judy?

(*Answers in her voice, badly:*) 'I-I-I sure have, Mr Say!'

How about you, Marilyn?

'Too too true, boo boo be-doo.'

LV: Don't.

RAY: No, seriously, LV, it'll never happen again, not with this.

(*Brandishes the notes:*) It's foolproof, believe me. Let's do it, eh?

She shakes her head.

Won't even look at it?

And again.

Well, if that's what you want.

LV: 'tis.

RAY (*thinking all the time*): Fair enough, I've got my other acts, I'll be all right,

I'll survive. And so will you. It's just that . . .

(*Looks at paper once more:*) Well, never mind . . . never mind then . . .

That's that, eh. No problem. Pas de problemo.

He folds the paper and pockets it. He wanders around, LV *watching him closely.* RAY *looks casual, but he's scheming hard. He wanders over to her record collection.*

RAY: You've got it nice in here, haven't you?

All clean and tidy.

All your records round you, eh?

That's nice.

Your dad must have spent years building up a
collection like this.

LV: 'e did.

RAY: I were never one for collecting things, meself.
Only debts.

He smiles, but he's working overtime.

(*Finally, an idea:*) I had an auntie once who was,
though.

You'll never guess what she collected.

Go on?

He approaches her bed and sits next to her, close.

Bluebirds.

Honest.

Wild bluebirds.

Flying all round her house.

Marvellous with them she was, n'all.

She even taught one of them to talk once.

LV *is slowly being sucked in.*

RAY: Yeah. Timid little thing it were.

No bigger than your thumb.

Too scared to even leave its cage.

And the way she did it was so simple.

All she did was keep it shaded and safe at all times . . .

Sing to it while stroking it, very soft, every day.

And after a while . . . it gave her its heart.

And later, when it'd grown strong . . . she set it free.

But . . . before it flew to freedom, it stopped on the
window ledge . . .

He points to LV*'s window ledge.*

Stopped still, and then . . . turned to her.

And . . . to her great surprise . . . sang.

(*Sings:*) 'There'll be blue birds over, the white cliffs of
Dover . . .'

See? There she goes.

They watch, as if they see it fly away.

56

RAY *taps* LV *and smiles.*

Pause.

Which were your dad's favourites then?

LV (*points to a pile*): Them three there.

RAY: Ahh.

Goes to get pen and paper out of his pocket, then . . .

Oh . . . no.

LV: What?

RAY: Well, I was thinking . . . we could've made sure we got them in, you know . . .

The Act.

But we're not doing it now.

Puts paper back but notices LV *doesn't say no.*

Bet he would've liked that though, your dad, eh?

Tribute to his life's loves?

One love, his songs, performed by his only other, his daughter.

Eh?

That would've really been something, wouldn't it?

Shame.

'Cos let's face it, the man and his music . . . they don't get much respect, do they?

If you know what I mean.

He indicates downstairs. Then he waits for it. It comes:

LV: Ray . . . ?

RAY (*casual*): Mm?

LV (*long pause, then*): Nothing.

RAY (*thrown, but then . . .*): Whup, look, there she goes again. The Bluebird.

Under the moon, look, and over the stars.

RAY *flutters his hand like dad used to. The hand's flightpath trails wickedly up and past the photo of dad.* LV *follows it and stares at the photo. Again* RAY *waits for it, and again it comes:*

LV: I'll do it.

57

RAY (*casually*): Do what?

    . . . Oh that, oh right, OK.

LV: Just once.

RAY (*managing to contain himself*): Yeah, whatever,
whatever.

    I'm pleased.

    I'll just nip downstairs for me cigarillos.

    Back in a sec.

RAY *calmly leaves the room . . .*

INT. LANDING. HOUSE. NIGHT.

*. . . and then, outside, like a proper bastard, releases his greedy
joy in a clench-fisted touchdown celebration to the thunderous
opening of:*

    'Goldfinger' – by Shirley Bassey

which carries over the following montage:

EXT. RAY'S CAR. TOWN. DAY.

*A classic postcard shot of the seaside town is carved in two as the
Cadillac swoops through frame.* RAY *motors at a slow but
menacing pace. We see a greedy determination in his eye. He is
busy on his mobile phone.*

EXT. MR BOO'S CLUB. DAY

RAY *arrives outside* MR BOO's *club where a team of*
WORKMEN *are waiting. As* RAY *leads them inside he is already
describing what he wants altering on the frontage of the club.*

INT. MR BOO'S CLUB. DAY.

Leading them into the club, RAY *continues his lengthy*

58

instructions, pointing to the stage, this here, that there etc. Like
Las Vegas.

SOUNDTRACK: *Goldfinger, he's the man, the man with the*
Midas touch
A spider's touch.

INT. LITTLE VOICE'S BEDROOM. DAY.
LV *is cleaning her records. A shiver goes through her.*

INT. MR BOO'S CLUB. DAY.
The workmen tell RAY *how much the job's going to cost. It's more*
than he expected.

INT. PAWN SHOP. DAY.
RAY *adds his watch to the pile of medallions on the counter*
between him and a PAWNBROKER, *then reluctantly forces a*
gold ring off his cold finger. He looks a tad disappointed with the
valuation.

SOUNDTRACK: *Such a Cold Finger, beckons you to enter his*
web of sin
But don't go in.

INT. BANK. DAY.
RAY *stares nastily at a shrugging* LOAN ADVISER, *who holds*
his hand out to shake but RAY *just walks out.*

SOUNDTRACK: *Golden words he will pour in your ear . . .*

EXT. HARBOUR. FISHERIES. DAY

The uniformed MARI *and* SADIE *go round the* WORKFORCE *doing a collection in a bucket labelled 'LV Concert Appeal'.* MARI *is apprehensive.*

SOUNDTRACK: *. . . but his lies can't disguise what you fear . . .*

INT. MR BOO'S CLUB. DAY.

MARI *walks through the club. Behind her we see the club going through change, a catwalk structure being added, backdrops and curtains being hung, new spotlights being erected etc., people everywhere.* MARI *meets* RAY *and tips out a heavy bagful of change and notes. He kisses her.*

SOUNDTRACK: *For a golden girl knows when he's kissed her,*
it's the kiss of death from Mr Goldfinger

INT. BOOKIES. DAY.

RAY *puts the bagful of change on a horse, which he promptly and sadly watches fail. He chucks his betting slip away.*

SOUNDTRACK: *Pretty girl, beware of his heart of gold . . .*
This heart is Cold.

INT. CLOTHES SHOP. DAY

MARI *and* SADIE *fuss over the bemused and increasingly unenthusiastic* LV *as she steps repeatedly out of a changing room in showbizzy dresses. On the final dress,* MARI *takes a flash photo of the startled* LV.

SOUNDTRACK: *Golden words he will pour in your ear,*
but his lies can't disguise what you fear . . .

60

INT. PRINTERS. DAY.
Posters of LITTLE VOICE *are churning out of a print machine.*

INT/EXT. SPA OPEN-AIR CONCERT HALL. DAY.
We see one of the hurriedly printed posters of 'Little Voice – Voice of a Thousand Stars' being slapped on to the glass frontage of the Vitadome. It features the startled photo from the previous scene. Doing the slapping are MARI *and* SADIE. *Behind them, inside the concert hall, we see* RAY *talking to a* BAND LEADER *while his band play to a handful of wind-battered old biddies in deckchairs. He too obviously mentions money. Rather a lot of it.* RAY *swallows hard but still indicates he'll see him straight.*

SOUNDTRACK: *For a golden girl knows when he's kissed her,*
                . . . it's the kiss of death . . . from Mr . . .

INT. FRONT ROOM. HOUSE. DAY.
Close-up of LV, *still little more than disinterested, as she watches* SADIE *and the obviously drunk* MARI *doing Shirley Bassey moves.* SADIE *stops a second to shove in a very un-Shirley-esque double-decker jam sandwich. While she does so* MARI *stares at* LV. *There is an unspoken, uneasy tension between the two.*

SOUNDTRACK: *Goldfinger, pretty girl beware of his heart of*
                gold . . .

EXT. TOWN. DAY.
Posters are being splashed up all over town.

EXT. SECOND-HAND CAR DEALERS. DAY.
Close-up of RAY *sitting in his car looking bitterly rueful. He is*

handed a thick brown envelope. A wide shot reveals a Second Hand Car Dealers. RAY *gets out of the car and some* SPIV *takes his place.* RAY *walks away, sadder but still determined, towards . . .*

SOUNDTRACK: *This heart is cold . . .*

INT. BOOKIES. DAY.
The thick brown envelope goes on another loser. An even more desperate RAY*, body and face even more sadly contorted as he sees his horse amble home after all the others. This time he is too stunned even to tear up his betting slip. He can't believe what he's just done.*

SOUNDTRACK: *He loves only gold . . . Only gold . . .*

INT. AMUSEMENT ARCADE. DAY.
A tiny but particularly evil-looking MONEYLENDER *witnesses* RAY*'s signature on a debt contract. Even big* RAY *looks lightweight as he is flanked by two enormous* BRUISERS. *He tries to smile.*

SOUNDTRACK: *He loves gold . . . He loves only gold . . . Only gold . . .*

INT. LITTLE VOICE'S BEDROOM. NIGHT.
LV *stares at the photo of her father, who still stares back.*

EXT. MR BOO'S CLUB. DAY.
RAY *pays off the several* WORKMEN *as they exit the club's main door.* RAY *follows them down the steps into close-up. He looks up*

62

proudly at the front of the club, full of jazzy neon. He clears
frame and they begin to glow as we mix to night:

SOUNDTRACK: *He loves GOLD!!*

EXT. MR BOO'S CLUB. NIGHT.
The jazzy lights flow spectacularly all over the front of the
previously drab Boo's Club, Las Vegas style. It is an astounding
(and obviously frighteningly expensive) transformation.
LITTLE VOICE.

INT. FRONT ROOM. HOUSE. NIGHT.
SADIE, *wearing a real Friday Night Frock, is helping* MARI *zip*
up into an ultra-tight black mini-dress.

MARI: A Man with a Plan or what, eh? My Ray?
　　Worked it all out he has and he's taking us all to Tarby-
　　land. Must say I had me doubts about her doing it
　　again but, well, he's won me over . . . Try as I do, I
　　cannot say no to that man.
　　She waltzes over to the bar to pour herself a drink. RAY
　　creeps in through the door. With her back to the door,
　　MARI *doesn't see him. He puts a 'ssh' sign up to* SADIE
　　and creeps up on MARI, *holding a necklace ready to put*
　　round her neck.
MARI: What a tongue he has on him, though, eh?
　　Half raspberry, half razor.
　　Oh, I don't know, Sade . . .
　　Maybe for once that fucker Fate is smiling down on us.
　　She has hair lacquer in one hand, gin in the other.
　　Ooh, liquor, lacquer, liquor, lacquer . . .
MARI *suddenly sprays lacquer. It goes in* RAY's *eyes.*
RAY: Aaargh!! Blood-y hell!!

63

MARI: Wha . . . Oh my God, I've blinded me God!

RAY (*scrunches his eyes*): I'm all right, I'm all right . . .
Here, I got you something. (*Holds out the necklace.*)

MARI: Oh, Raymondo!! (*She puts it on.*)
Looky here, little sparkle-neck me!
See, Sade? A love token, that's it, in't it, Ray!
RAY, *wiping his eyes with a dirty tea-towel, nods.*

MARI: In some ways I wish I could lash it round me finger.

RAY (*hastily changes the subject, still in pain*): Hey, Sadie,
you're looking stunning tonight, love.
We gonna get a dance down there later then, eh?
SADIE *laughs a peculiar snorted laugh.* MARI *jumps in
quickly:*

MARI: Sadie, go upstairs now, see if star turn's ready.

RAY: Can't wait, Mari, can you?
I'm buzzing fit to burst, me.
Big crowd, proper job.
Even got a talent scout to come down.

MARI: Ey, give us your lips, you, and double me palpitations.
She goes to kiss him, but his attention is grabbed by LV,
standing at the doorway in front of SADIE. *She wears a
long, figure-hugging, sparkling cabaret dress which stretches
to the floor. The effect is dazzling. Especially in these
surroundings.* RAY *freezes.* MARI *is kissing him but he
doesn't even notice.*

RAY (*under his breath*): Fuck me.

MARI: Not now, Ray, we got a show to do . . . Haa . . . !
Her laugh stops halfway through as she sees LV *sparkling
in the doorway. They all stare at her as if they've never
seen her before. Which they haven't, not like this. A stunned
appreciative silence.*

MARI (*out of the limelight-ish*): Right, are we set then or what?
RAY *rushes to the door as* SADIE *drapes a pink plastic mac
over* LV*'s shoulders.*

RAY: Let me open that door! The door that leads to success!

A beam of spotlight hits MR BOO. *A big cheer from a big Friday crowd. The club interior feels totally different. It is more crowded, more plush, tables have lights on, the stage looks more Caesar's Palace than working men's club.* MR BOO *stands at the frontstage mike.*

MR BOO: Welcome welcome welcome, yea, thrice welcome, to Mr Boo's.
Knock knock?
'Who's there?'
Boo!
'Boo Who?'
Oh, don't be so fucking pathetic!
So how're you doing, then, all reet?
Muted response.
Oh, come on you can do better than that,
HOW ARE YOU ALL DOING, ALL REET?!
More enthusiasm.
That's more like it, because we've pulled out all 'stops for your Friday night frolickings.
We haven't had a band this big in here since VE day.
In fact, it's the same band by 'looks of it.
It's all right, they know me.
So smack one hand against the other if you will . . .
For the Turn Of Turns' Return,
The Voice of a Thousand Stars,
The Girl with the Greats queueing up in her Gullet.
A-the one, a-the only . . .
LITTLE VOICE, ladies and gentlemen!!
(*Brazilian goal style*): LIIIIIII-TTLLLEE-VOOOIIIICCCEEE!!!
BOO *spreads an arm showbiz-style and backsteps nattily offstage. The curtains open as the audience applauds loudly and encouragingly. A huge bell-shaped cage, like a*

65

birdcage, sits centre stage. Spotlights hit it from all sides. In it we see a petrified LV. *The stage is all gold trims and blue curtains, everything about the club is suddenly glam. In the middle of this huge investment,* LV *turns and faces the audience. Possessed. There are cheers of encouragement, but eventually the applause dies down to a silence. An uneasy silence.* LV *steps down from the cage and nervously, very nervously, walks to the front of the stage. The painfully uncomfortable pause continues as her eyes again scan the crowd. Silence. Pause. A worried conductor. We see* RAY – *terrified –* MARI *fearful. We see* LV *in close-up, searching the audience. We see her POV, the staring faces, expectation on each one. The odd shout for her to do something. Then her eyes suddenly light up. We see her POV: The* MAN, *sitting at a table at the back, lifts his head and smiles. A wave of confidence swells in* LV, *her whole body language changes and – as* RAY *exhales his relief and like everyone, becomes transfixed – she becomes Shirley Bassey:*

'Big Spender'

LV: 'The minute you walked in the joint,
    I could see you were a man of distinction,
    a real big spender.
    Good-looking, so refined, say wouldn't you like to know
    what's going on in my mind?'
The audience is impressed, the band is impressed, but most importantly for LV, *the* MAN *is impressed. Suddenly gaining a confidence we haven't seen from her,* LV *begins gradually to do all the Bassey actions. She's thrilling, she's funny, but you can see it in her eyes, she is almost unaware of what she's doing.*

LV: 'So let me get right to the point:
    I don't pop my cork for every man I see
    Hey big spender, hey big spender, hey big spender,

spennnnd a little time with me-eeee! Yes! . . .'
It is stunning, amazing, and sends the crowd into raptures
of applause. Clapping with the rest we see the proud
SADIE, *the surprised* MR BOO, *the astonished* MARI, *the*
gobsmacked GEORGE *and the told-you-so* RAY. *The* MAN
smiles warmly. We see a mixed montage of the whole show,
the camera swirling round LV, *cutting back and forth*
between the band, the crowd, the interested parties, and
especially between her and her approving father. Always,
from a distance, LV *looks spectacularly confident, but again*
and again, we see in her close-ups that there is that
haunted, passionate, possessed look in her eye. A single spot
on LV*'s white face, coy, sexy, Marilyn Monroe. She stares*
directly at the MAN. *Another perfect impression.*

'I Wanna Be Loved By You'

LV: 'I wanna be loved by you, nobody else but you
     I wanna be loved by you, alo-one . . . boo-boo bi doo.
     I wanna be kissed by you,
     just you, and nobody else but you,
     I wanna be kissed by you. Alone.
     I couldn't aspire to anything higher
     Than to feel the desire to make you my own
     b-doom b-doom b-doom b-dum boo
     I wanna be loved by you, just you and nobody else but
     you,
     I wanna be loved by you
     Tiddly tiddly tiddly tum, boo boo bi-doo.'
Laughter and applause. Mix to:
     LV *looking pale and Germanic among the club smoke.*
Marlene Dietrich:

'Falling In Love Again'

LV: 'Men cluster to me like moths around ze flame
     and if zeir winks burn I know I'm not to blame

Fallink in luff again
Vot am I to do, never vonted to
I can't help it.'
More laughter, cheers.

   Mix to:

   LV, *marching on the spot, suddenly brassy, strident:*
Gracie Fields: The crowd clap in time:

'*Sing As We Go*'

LV: 'Sing as we go, and let the world go by
Singing a song we march along the highway
Say goodbye to sorrow,
there's always tomorrow, to think of today.
Sing as we go although the skies are grey
Beggar or king, you've got to sing a gay tune
A song and a smile making life worthwhile
So sing, o-a-o-a-a-o-a, as we go along.'
Huge cheers.

   Mix to:

   LV, *seeing her dad's pleasure, full wind in her sails now,*
the moves and voice of Judy Garland. Perhaps even more
than everyone else, RAY *claps along enthusiastically.*
Special lights flash, glitter tumbles from above the stage.
Euphoria everywhere. Starting with thundering drums, an
especially upbeat and spectacular brass backing to:

'*Get Happy*'

LV: 'Forget your troubles, get happy, your cares fly away . . .
Shout Hallelujah, get happy, get ready, for your . . .
Judgement DAY come on get happy
Chase your cares away
Shout Hallelujah c'mon get happy
Get ready for the judgement day
Sun is shining c'mon get happy
Lord is waiting to take your hand

68

Hallelujah, c'mon, get happy
We're going to the promised land
Heading cross the river,
wash your sins away in the tide,
It's all so peaceful on the other side . . .'
Among the crowd we see a TALENT SCOUT *at a table,*
holding his mobile phone up to the stage and crowd like a
microphone. RAY *spots him, and goes over to him.*
RAY: Who's that on the phone?
SCOUT: It's Bunny Morris.
RAY: 'Bunny Morris'!?

INT. BUNNY MORRIS'S OFFICE. LONDON. NIGHT.
The camera tracks past a wall full of posters and signed framed
photographs of successful television and showbiz personalities,
and ends on the smart-suited BUNNY MORRIS *sitting listening*
down the phone at his enormous desk. He's loving it.

INT. BOO'S SHOW CLUB. NIGHT.
The crowd excitement builds towards the end of the song. Now
RAY *is holding up the mobile phone.*

LV (*big big finish*):
'Shout Hallelujah come on get happy
You better chase all your cares away
Shout Hallelujah come on get happy
Get ready . . . get ready . . . get ready . . . !
For the judgement da-aay!!'
A huge, spectacular finale, the audience rises as one to its
feet. A great great show. As the applause crashes in LV
looks vainly for her father, but there is no sign of him now.
Just an empty table. She looks down, drained, exhausted,
sad. The crowd continues to go wild, even after the curtain

drops on the static, from LV.

EXT. PIGEON HILL. NIGHT.
BILLY, *still waiting in the night for Duane, hears the distant
roar from the club.*

INT. BOO'S SHOW CLUB. NIGHT.
Later. The stage lights are down, house lights up. MARI, SADIE
and BOO *celebrate at one of the tables. Everyone else has gone.*
LV *sits perched, drained, on the frame of the birdcage on the now
darkened stage.* RAY *arrives at the table, barely controlling a
dance in his step.* MR BOO *pops open a bottle of champagne.*

MR BOO: Well, A Star is bloody Born or what?
RAY: Guess who I just spoke to then? Only Bunny Morris.
MR BOO: Never!
MARI (*whoops knowledgably, then*): Who's Bunny Morris?
RAY: The fixer! Bunny Mr Starmaker Morris!
　　　Any new star you name, love, Bunny got them started.
　　　Gets them in at all the big clubs, on all the TV shows.
　　　If he rates them, that's it.
　　　No one says no to Bunny Morris. And neither did I . . .
　　　He's only coming down to see her tomorrow night!
MR BOO: No!
RAY: Honest! He is! Coming here!
　　　Picking him up at the Grand at seven . . .
MARI: Tomorrow? We on tomorrow n'all?
LV (*shakes head slowly*): Once . . . was said.
　　　No one hears her.
MR BOO: Aye, I've cancelled the Silverados and Gringo
　　　Hodges. Had to. They were going mad in here tonight.
RAY: Tell you, when Bunny sees her he'll do the same.
　　　Then that'll be it, we'll never be off the telly.
70

MFI Friday, Letterman, the *100, he'll* fix them all.

LV: Just once . . . we said.

> *Still no one hears.* LV *starts to wilt slightly, in an exhausted trance.*

RAY: What did I tell you, love?

Today this crap-house, tomorrow the bloody world.

Route bloody one. London, Leeds, Las Vegas!

> MARI *lets out another American whoop.*

MR BOO: Aye, well, I hope you'll not forget where you got your start, Ray. My crap-house.

And you know what they say . . .

Shouldn't shit on folk on 'way up 'cos you're bound to meet them on 'way down.

RAY: Yeah, but we're not coming down, Boo.

Up to the sky we're going.

Up to the bloody sky!

Here's to the rise and rise of Little Voice..

> *They all stand, turn and raise their glasses 'cheers' to* LV *who promptly falls off the cage and crashes to the stage. They stare, stunned stock still for a moment.*

EXT. MR BOO'S CLUB. NIGHT.

A wide shot sees the bright 'LITTLE VOICE' sign flicker off as the doors are crashed open by SADIE *who tenderly, protectively, carries* LV *in her big arms.* MARI *is in close attendance.* MR BOO *and* RAY *follow.*

MARI: Oh, God . . . The little bird's bleated and died with all the shock!

RAY: She's all right Mari. Just tired . . . bright lights and all that.

MR BOO (*to* RAY): 'Blessed are the meek for they shall inherit the earth.'

But when, eh? When?

RAY *looks at him, 'Eh?'*

MR BOO: Don't push her too hard, will you, Ray?

RAY: (*watches* MARI *and* SADIE *carry* LV): She needs
pushing, Mr Boo, that's the point.

MR BOO: Aye, just, I've seen a lot of big talent wasted in my
time.

RAY: Oh don't come the fucking impresario with me, Boo.
You run a club nobody in their right mind goes to.
Tell jokes nobody in their right mind laughs at.
You're a nothing, Boo.
It's me with the contacts now.
Me with friends in high places.
Remember that, eh, it's Ray who's the big shot now.

MR BOO (*stung, recovers*): You lot need a ride home?

BOO *nods to* RAY*'s old Cadillac across the car park.*

MR BOO: May not have friends in high places, Ray.
But I've got 'em in the fucking motor trade.
Fade out.

EXT. SHIPLEY STREET. DAY.

BILLY *stands in the street below* LV*'s window. He cups his
hands and shouts up.*

BILLY: LV! LV! I know you're there, LV.
I've been by 'club.
You did it again, didn't you, and again tonight it
says.
LV! I'm worried LV, are you all right?
Just . . . don't let them do it to you.
LV? I know you're there . . . I just want to . . .
He suddenly stops as he sees, on the roof above
LV*'s window, a* PIGEON. *A familiar one.*
. . . Duane . . . ?

72

The window is flung open and Duane flies off, frightened.
MARI *leans angrily out of the window.*
MARI: Ey, fuck off, Romeo!
　　You wanna see her? Then sod off down club and
　　pay like everyone else.
　　The window slams shut.

INT. LITTLE VOICE'S BEDROOM. DAY.
MARI *composes herself at the window. Turns.*

MARI: Can do without that sort of crap just before show, eh?
　　When you need to be . . . concentrating yer mind.
　　The camera reveals things aren't quite that up-to-schedule.
　　LV *is a motionless shape under her bedclothes.* SADIE *sits*
　　next to her on the bed, one hand on LV*'s head, the other*
　　holding a plate bearing a long-ignored sandwich.
MARI: Oh, come on, love, enough of this, eh?
　　You've not opened your beak all day, to eat or to
　　squeak.
　　I mean, even you squeak from time to time, don't you?
　　Oh, LV, love, am I to get doctor?
　　Oh, come on, love, squeak to me, eh?
　　MARI *squeaks at* LV *in encouragement, then looks at her*
　　with growing but stifled anger. Then at her bedside clock.
　　Feels sick with fear.

INT/EXT. PIGEON HILL. DAY.
BILLY *walks carefully up to his loft and looks in. Duane is in his*
open cage. He closes it with a smile. Then looks at his watch.

EXT. MR BOO'S CLUB. NIGHT.
The camera pans down from the frontage and its additional text:

Back By Popular Demand

as RAY *and* BUNNY *step out of a taxi and walk towards the club.*

BUNNY: Long time since I were dragged down to the
    northern clubs, Say, she'd better be good . . .
    (*Then, suddenly, understandably impressed by the glitz:*)
    . . . Bloody hell.
    RAY *smiles and leads* BUNNY *in. As they clear frame we*
    see BILLY, *apprehensive, uncertain whether to go in or not.*
    GEORGE *appears, arm in arm with a* WOMAN.
GEORGE: Now then, thought you'd show up here sooner or
    later. You going in?
BILLY: Er . . . dunno. Hi, you must be George's wife?
WOMAN: 'Wife. . . .'? . . . You bastard.
    She kicks GEORGE's *leg and storms off.* GEORGE *looks*
    up to the heavens.
GEORGE: For one not known for his overusage of words,
    you don't half pick 'em, do you?
    (*Sighs, annoyed:*) Spare ticket now if you want one.

INT. LITTLE VOICE'S BEDROOM. NIGHT.
LV *is still motionless in bed, alone in her room. We hear the*
approaching voice of MARI, *more desperate and irritable with*
time, as she comes up the stairs with SADIE.

MARI: No, she's not moved, Sadie, love.
    But she's going to have to in a minute.
    Otherwise she'll be going on as she is.
    I bet that Judy Garland never went onstage in her
    sodding jim-jams, so I don't know why she wants to.
    They enter, all spangly-dressed ready for a glittery night out.
    Oh, come on, LV, whatever's bugging you just let it
    stop, eh?
74

Just for a few hours, eh?

'Cos look, we're cutting things a bit fine now,

Ray'll be here in a minute and your mam's getting a

little bit . . . *fucking irate, all right?*

Oh, Jesus, Sadie, look at the bloody time.

We hear a drum roll.

Cut to:

INT. MR BOO'S SHOW CLUB. NIGHT.

The packed house hushes in anticipation. Lights go down.

MC (*off*): Ladies and gentlemen!

Will you welcome please on this night of all nights, the

compere of all comperes . . . the world's *finest* MC, and

funniest man never to have been on television . . .

Backstage, we see that the fantastic introduction to MR

BOO *is in fact being given by* MR BOO *himself, standing*

with a mike in the wings.

MR BOO . . . The man the *Northern Echo* called 'quite

amusing'. The chuckle-bag himself . . . Your very

own . . .

MIII-IISTER BOOOOO!

Big-band intro music, loud applause, as MR BOO *jogs*

confidently on to the stage. He has dug out of his collection

the most spectacular tux he can find in the desperate hope of

catching BUNNY MORRIS*'s eye. This is his big chance as*

well as RAY*'s, and he's going for it.*

MR BOO: Welcome welcome welcome.

Yea, thrice welcome, friends, to Mr Boo's.

I am Mr Boo, don't shout out my name or I'll think you

don't like me. Ha!

A small laugh, things are looking up.

Now have we got some entertainment for you tonight?

I don't know . . .

75

(*To wings:*) . , Have we got some entertainment for
them tonight?
Yes we have, of course we have.
And we all know what that entertainment is, don't we?
'Cos tonight, for the second consecutive night . . . in a
row, sees the return of young Little Voice.
There are cheers. BUNNY MORRIS *is somewhat taken
aback by the support.* BILLY *looks on nervously.*

MR BOO: But that's all in the future . . . that's to look
forward to.

INT/EXT. TAXI. NIGHT.
RAY *sits in the back of the taxi, cracking his knuckles nervously.*
Takes a shot from his hip flask.

INT. LITTLE VOICE'S BEDROOM. NIGHT.
MARI *paces back and forth frantically.*

MARI: Oh, Ray's going to kill me, he's going to throttle
me . . .
Then what'd you be like, eh? With me murdered?
Be up and about then, happy as a lark I suppose.
She crosses to the window.
No bloody crooning for your dead mam, oh no,
oh no . . . oh no he's here, he's *here* . . .
We see her POV of jazzy RAY *stepping out of the waiting
taxi. In a panic,* MARI *pushes* SADIE *to one side and grabs
hold of* LV, *shaking her. She is like a floppy lifeless puppet.*

MARI: Oh, Jesus Jesus, come on, LV, please . . . do it for yer
mam? Do something for *me* for a change, eh?
Instead of that lousy dopey drip *of a dead dad! Fuck!*
*She throws her back on to the bed and storms out of the
room.*

76

INT. FRONT ROOM. HOUSE. NIGHT.

RAY *comes in through the door and heads straight for a bottle.*
MARI *comes rushing down the stairs and into the front room.*
RAY *is restless with nervous tension. Cat on a hot tin roof.* MARI
throws her arms round him as he guzzles a whisky.

MARI: Darling!
RAY: All right, Mari, OK.
  Ooh, bloody hell, girl, this is it, eh?
  Where is she then?
  All right, LV? Management is here!
MARI: Er, Ray, love, there's a . . . bit of a . . .
  LV, she's dead tired, Ray, she's really not . . .
RAY: Aren't we all, love, eh?
  Be all right when she's up there.
  SADIE *appears in the doorway.* MARI *pulls hard on her*
  cigarette.

INT. MR BOO'S SHOW CLUB. NIGHT.

MR BOO: So now, ladies and gentlemen, time for our first
  act. Five lads from Grimsby who have a history of
  touching arseholes . . . 'Our souls', I said, madam, 'our
  souls'.
  Big laughter, like heaven to BOO.
  The biggest thing in rock: Take Fat!
  Raunchy music introduces the huge flabby fivesome who
  bound on to the stage in the tightest of leather briefs. The
  crowd cheers, BUNNY *gapes in disbelief, a fish out of*
  water. BILLY *is nervous, uneasy in the crowd, not*
  laughing like GEORGE *alongside him.*

INT. FRONT ROOM. HOUSE. NIGHT.

MARI *is panicking more now, still unable to break the news to* RAY.

MARI: Ray . . . ? Ray . . . can she not have this night off?

RAY (*laughs, sits down in a chair*): This night off? What you
  on about? Bunny Morris is there. There, now, waiting.
  This night off! This night!?
  This is THE night, love!
  *Turns on lamp which POPS! He spills drink on suit and
  rubs hand.*
  Fucking house . . . !
  He jumps up and prowls again.

MARI: Ray . . . ?

RAY (*increasingly irritated*): Ray Ray Ray *What?*
  MARI *is surprised by his irritation.*

RAY: You get her dress from dry-cleaners OK, yeah?

MARI: (*gulp, pause, then pass*): Sadie love? You pick up the
  dress?
  SADIE *hasn't a clue.*

RAY: Oh no, you fucking forgot it . . . oh, Jesus
  CHRIST!!

MARI: I've been so busied with her, Ray . . .
  RAY *kicks a cheap occasional table.*

MARI: Hey, watch me furniture, you!

RAY: 'Furniture'!?

INT. BOO'S SHOW CLUB. NIGHT.

MR BOO: Ladies and gentlemen, a novelty act that's noveller
  than any I know.
  BUNNY'S *shoulders drop in dread.*

MR BOO: Please welcome, BRENDA BAILEY and her
  FARMYARD FROLICS!

The curtain rises and we see BRENDA *and her assorted farmyard animals.* GEORGE *groans,* BILLY *laughs at last.*

INT. FRONT ROOM. HOUSE. NIGHT.
RAY *pours himself another stiff whisky.* MARI *is clumsily trying to erect the ironing board.*

RAY: Two things, Mari, that's all you had to do.
　　Get her dress and have her ready. Two things!
　　And you've frigging well fucked up on *both!*
MARI: I know I know! Oh, I'm so sorry, darling . . .
　　(She goes to embrace him. Girlishly:) Don't be crossy wid
　　your rolling puss-puss.
RAY *(pushes her aside)*: Never mind all that crap.
　　RAY *is swigging with purpose now.*

INT. WINGS. BOO'S CLUB. NIGHT.
Side stage, MR BOO *is panicking. In the background, onstage, we can see* BRENDA *and her flapping farm-yarders. He sees* TRIGGER SMITH *limbering up with his knives alongside his octogenarian assistant* ELAINE. *Goes up to them.*

MR BOO: Have you seen Ray Say or LV?
　　TRIGGER *shakes his head.*
MR BOO: Christ . . .
　　Hey, Trigger . . . You'd better string it out a bit.
　　Do an extra five minutes, yeah?
TRIGGER *(a bright idea)*: Oh, right. Hey, I can do my
　　blindfold bit.
　　He indicates his neckerchief. ELAINE *emits a terrified whimper.*

79

INT. FRONT ROOM. HOUSE. NIGHT.

MARI *digs a crumpled dress out of the dirty clothes bin-liner.*

MARI: Here, Sadie, give that 'once-over with iron, eh?
SADIE: O-K.
RAY: What . . . she's not even dressed?
    What's going . . . ? Oh, we can't have this, Mari . . .
    I'm going to have to get someone else to look after her.
MARI: Ray . . . What are you on about?
    What are you saying? . . . Ray?
    RAY *turns his back on her, nastily, refills a glass. There is a*
    long silent pause. The world stands still as MARI *realises*
    what is happening. She pulls on her cigarette in
    desperation. Finally, she has to lash out, so she lashes out at
    the nearest easy target: SADIE.
MARI: Ey! You're too quiet to be me friend, you. FUCK
    OFF!!
    Stunned, bewildered, SADIE *puts the iron down and moves*
    slowly to the door. MARI *picks up the iron and goes to*
    work on the dress. She's crap at it, sliding all over the shop.
MARI: I'm doing it now, Ray, love, yes I am.
    RAY *still has his coldest shoulder towards her.*

INT. MR BOO'S CLUB. NIGHT.

MR BOO: Ladies and gents, please welcome . . .
    WILD TRIGGER SMITH AND THE LOVELY
    ELAINE!
    The curtain rises on shaky TRIGGER *and the already*
    spinning ELAINE. BOO *looks on apprehensively. The*
    crowd groan a little.

MARI *continues her hopeless attempt at ironing.* RAY *swigs off and puts down his final drink and marches at* MARI.

RAY: Leave it, Mari, we haven't got time.
She continues ironing frantically, he gets hold of her hand.
LEAVE IT!
and burns his hand on the iron.
Fuck! You . . . FUCK!

MARI (*grabs his hand*): Ray, Ray . . .

RAY (*it's the burnt one*): Oow! What? What!?

MARI: Kiss me, Ray.
She strains towards him.

RAY: Oh, give over, Mari, we haven't got the time.

MARI (*she clings on to him*): Ray?

RAY: (*he pushes her off him and on to the sofa*): Give up
clinging, will you?!
You're all over me all the time like the bloody pox.

MARI (*follows him again*): Oh, don't spoil it, Ray . . . We go
so well together.
She tries to hug him.

RAY: Go so *well* together!?? We go nowhere!
For a start, you're past it.
Your body's gone.
When your clothes go, I can't keep track of it.
It's all over the place.
There's no way you're coming with me and her to
better things.
No way, love.
LV, YOU'VE GOT TEN FUCKING SECONDS!

INT. LITTLE VOICE'S BEDROOM. NIGHT
Upstairs, the motionless LV *finally utters a tiny, private,
somewhat bizarre mumble. It is Marilyn Monroe:*

LV: 'I'm tired . . . of getting the fuzzy end of the lollipop.'

INT. FRONT ROOM. HOUSE. NIGHT.
RAY *takes a final swig of Scotch then turns and looks across at the shaken, dishevelled, sad* MARI. *He moves menacingly towards her.*

RAY: All you're doing is getting in the way.
You were in the way the first night I heard her, and you're still in the way now.
Christ, do you think I don't have birds I go to?
Don't you think it's like putting me face in *flowers* after you?
You've had it, Mari.
For God's sake wise up, woman, eh?
Eh? (*Face to face now, whispers:*) . . . and fuck off.
RAY *leaves her broken, shattered.*

INT. STAGE. MR BOO'S CLUB. NIGHT.
Thunk! As a knife slams into the spinning board, nearer to ELAINE*'s sweaty brow than planned.*

TRIGGER (*blindfolded*): Elaine? You still there?
In the wings, BOO *watches* TRIGGER *and* ELAINE *with growing concern.* BRENDA *too.*
BRENDA: Get them off, Boo, you go on, it's not right.
MR BOO: They're all right.
There is the whizz of a knife, a thunk like none before, slightly fleshy, and a scream. BOO*'s face drops.*
MR BOO: CURTAINS!!!
He pushes past BRENDA *and rushes on to the stage, ushering the blindfolded* TRIGGER *behind the fast closing curtains.*

82

Tar, thank you, tar . . .
Wild Trigger Smith and the lovely . . . lucky Elaine!

EXT. SHIPLEY STREET. NIGHT.
We hear the sound of an ambulance, presumably ELAINE*'s, as*
MARI *staggers out the house and across the road towards*
SADIE*'s.*

MARI: Sadie . . . *Sadie . . . !*
    SADIE *opens her door.*

INT. LITTLE VOICE'S BEDROOM. NIGHT.
LV *is still lying on her bed. The door crashes open.*

RAY: What you *doing!?* Here, get this on.
    He throws the dress at her.
    Come on, I've had enough of you lot tonight.
    LV *doesn't respond.*
RAY: Hey! Dress! On! *Now!*
    And still doesn't.
    MOVE, will you!!
    He grabs her. She's limp in his arms. He slaps her. Hard.
    Suddenly, voices begin to rush out of her. Some sung, some
    spoken, but all uncontrollably.
LV (*Cilla Black, as in* Blind Date): 'Hello number one, what's
    yer name and where d'yer come from?'
RAY: Wha . . . ?
LV (*Judy Garland, as in* A Star Is Born): 'This is Mrs . . .
    Norman . . . Maine.'
RAY: Hey, stop messing, LV, come on, quick, we're *late!* . . .
LV (*Gracie Fields*): '. . . So hurry up before they shut the
    gate . . .
RAY: Look, save it for the punters . . .

83

LV (*Gracie Fields*): 'Click clack click clack click clack click
There's music in the clatter of the clogs.'
*She is off the bed now, forcing him across the room with the
verbal torrent.*

RAY: Hey, stop it now, LV . . .

LV (*Judy Garland*): 'I know, I'll sing 'em all and we'll stay all
night!'

RAY (*raises a hand*): LV, I'm warning you . . .

LV: (*Marilyn Monroe*): 'My heart belongs to Daddy'.
RAY *slaps her, hard.*

LV: (*Marilyn Monroe*, Some Like It Hot): 'See what I mean?
Not very bright!''
RAY *laughs, nervously.*

LV (*Gracie Fields*): 'But the villain only laughed! He-he-he-
hee!'

RAY (*really worried now*): Hey, now . . . LV . . . Come on . . .
*She advances on him, forcing him out on to the landing as
the verbal stream increases.*

LV: (*Shirley Bassey*): 'When you smile smile smile smile
smile smile smile'
(*Judy Garland*): 'Toto! Toto! Run Toto run!'

INT. HALLWAY. HOUSE. NIGHT.
LV *has forced* RAY *down her stairs and across the hall.*

RAY: LV, don't . . . crack now . . . we're on our way
together . . .

LV (*Judy Garland*): 'Happy together, unhappy together . . .'
RAY *is backing off now with the sheer force of it. She's
demonic. She forces him to the door near the top of the stairs
to the shop.*

RAY: LV . . . please! Why . . . ?

LV (*Munchkin*): 'Because because because because because
because of the wonderful things he does.'

84

Again he raises his hand to hit her.

RAY: I warned you . . .

But LV *gets in first with a scratch of the Lion's face à la* Wizard of Oz:

LV (*Judy Garland*): 'Shame on you!!'

> *She scratches his nose. He topples backwards, loses his balance and crashes down the stairs, hitting the sides as he goes. He crumples in a heap at the bottom. Under a cut eyebrow, he looks up to* LV *at the top of the stairs: He holds his jaw.*

LV (*Gracie Fields*): Never mind yer teeth, leave 'em out!

INT. DOWNSTAIRS SHOP. NIGHT.

RAY *kicks the door open and starts to rush out. As he pulls himself through the door he grabs hold of wiring on the wall which breaks and sparks as he does so. He leaves the shop. Behind him, a shooting flash runs like lightning up a wire to the ceiling . . .*

INT. HALLWAY. NIGHT.

. . . and through the floor behind LV. *A plug socket bursts into flames behind her. She turns. And sees another, distant, plug flash.*

LV (*Judy Garland*): 'Lions and tigers and bears, oh my! Lions and tigers and bears . . . oh my!'

> *From the kitchen we hear a loud bang and a smoking piece of coat-hanger drops into frame. Lights are popping out all over the house. Wires flash and spark everywhere. We see* LV*'s face lit by these sparks.*

LV (*Judy Garland*): 'I'm frightened, Auntie Em, I'm frightened . . .'

MR BOO: (*off*) Ey, now we're cooking, aren't we!

INT. MR BOO'S SHOW CLUB. NIGHT.
But the crowd by now have been stunned into silence by the lack
of entertainment. MR BOO *is not helping things either, by his*
repertoire of jokes of which he's forgotten the end.

MR BOO: So anyway, this chicken goes into a library in
　　　Essex . . . No . . . hold up . . . no . . . it wasn't a chicken,
　　　was it . . . er . . .
　　　Um . . .
　　　He sees nothing but BUNNY MORRIS*'s appalled*
　　　expression
　　　Er . . . oh pff . . . It's gone . . .
　　　He dries. The crowd get extremely restless.

INT. HALLWAY. HOUSE. NIGHT.
Real flames now in the hall. LV, *trance-like, returns slowly up*
the stairs towards her room, singing as the fire grows in the
foreground.

LV: (*Marilyn Monroe*): 'Don't let the flames go out, some
　　　like it hot!'
　　　She closes her bedroom door, on which are the plastic
　　　initials LV.

INT. MR BOO'S. NIGHT.
Things have taken a turn for the worse, the turn being MR
BOO*'s. The natives are angry, shouting for him to get off,*
shouting for LV *to come on. He's sweating. A bored* BUNNY *is*
thinking of leaving. So is a concerned BILLY.

MR BOO: . . . yes, she's a red-head, my wife. No hair, just a
　　　red head. No, I love her terribly, I do. That's what she
　　　says anyway . . .

86

Looks to wings, desperate. Gets a shake of a head.
Now look, calm down, she'll be ready in a sec.
Now what did I tell you, eh?
If you didn't laugh at my jokes I'd sing, that's what I
said!
And Boo's a man of his word, I'm afraid.
BUNNY*'s had enough, he gets up and leaves.*

MR BOO: Bunny! Bunny, bear with me . . .
Anyway, as they say in the business . . .
'This . . . ladies and gentlemen . . . is me.'
(*Starts to sing, awfully:*) Your baby doesn't love you any
more'
(*Counts the surprised band in:*) Two, three, four . . .
And turns to see RAY *having suddenly appeared onstage
beside him, boozed up, bleeding, bedraggled and very very
bitter.*

MR BOO (*delighted, relieved*): Ray!!
RAY *punches him off the stage. The crowd 'ooh'.* BILLY *is
especially confused.* BUNNY *stops on his way out.* RAY
*stares at the stunned audience. The band have started the
intro to:*

'It's Over'

RAY: I 'ad something, ladies and . . . I had something really
special.

INT. LITTLE VOICE'S BEDROOM. NIGHT.
LV *has a petrified look under her trance. She is gathering all her
records, clutching them. There is a glow under the door. Smoke
begins to rise through the gaps in her wooden floor.*

LV (*Judy Garland*): 'This is my room . . . and I'm not
going to leave here ever ever again . . . because I love
you all.'

INT. MR BOO'S. NIGHT.

RAY *is distracted by the continuing repetitive intro and, unhinged as he is, he can't help but start to sing. He can't sing to save his life, but right now he reckons that's worth frig all anyway.* BILLY *leaves quickly.*

RAY: 'Golden days before they end'
　　　End? They never bloody started!
　　　Bunny Morris . . . Bunny Starmaker Morris!?
　　　Sees him leaving.
　　　Fuck off then, you jumped up little twat.
　　　'Your baby won't be near you, any more.'
　　　Good job, 'cos they always fuck it up for you, don't
　　　they?

EXT. CAR PARK. BOO'S CLUB. NIGHT.

BILLY *jumps into his cherry-picker and skids away.*

RAY (*off*): 'Tender nights before they fly'
　　　Well, mine has . . .
　　　'Send falling stars that seem to cry'
　　　. . . aye, 'cos they can't fucking *hack it.*

INT. BACK ROOM. SADIE'S HOUSE. NIGHT.

SADIE *sits next to* MARI *on the sofa watching high-volume TV.* MARI *is crying into a large gin while* SADIE *digs into a packet of crisps.* SADIE *offers a crisp to* MARI *who at last breathes in, then lets out a long painful wail.*

SADIE (*comforts her*): O-K.

INT. MR BOO'S. NIGHT.

RAY *staggers, the crowd gape. He flicks the mike lead, an attempt to look like a singer.*

RAY: Ladies and Gentlemen I had a dream
    'It's over.'
    When I think what might have been, eh?
    'It breaks your heart in two.'
    Finished, fucking finished, me.
    'To know she's been untrue.'

INT. HALLWAY. NIGHT.

Downstairs the phone is on fire. The sofa bursts into flames. Thick smoke now in the hallway. We see LV's bedroom door. Paint is bubbling. The letters are melting.

EXT. SHIPLEY STREET. NIGHT.

We see the house aglow. Flames lick the name above the door —
Francis Hoff.

INT. LITTLE VOICE'S BEDROOM. NIGHT.

LV *is madly muttering to herself as the corridor outside is ablaze.*

LV (*Judy Garland*): '. . . no place like home, there's no place
    like home.'

INT. MR BOO'S. NIGHT.

RAY: 'But oh what will you do?'
    What am I going to do, eh?
    He sees the nasty-looking MONEYLENDER *glaring at him*

89

from the back of the club, with his HEAVIES.
What the fuck am I going to do, eh? Eh? . . .
'WE'RE THROUGH!'

INT. BACK ROOM. SADIE'S HOUSE. NIGHT.
Almost ESP, SADIE *just senses something is happening outside.*
She gets up and moves slowly to the door. When she opens it, we
see the red glow reflected on her worried face, tinged with a blue
flashing light.

SADIE (*frozen panic*): OK . . . wha . . . ? O-K . . . O-K . . .

INT. MR BOO'S. NIGHT.

RAY: 'It's over'.

INT. LITTLE VOICE'S BEDROOM. NIGHT.
LV *sits on the floor among all the albums, clutching and looking*
at the picture of her father. The room is filling with smoke.

LV (*Judy Garland*): 'There's no place like home, there's no
    place . . .'
    The window smashes. BILLY *stands there on his cherry-*
    picker, his arms outstretched.
RAY (*off*): 'It's over!!'

EXT. SHIPLEY STREET. NIGHT.
Firemen have arrived. They train their hoses on the house as,
down through the smoke and spray, BILLY *brings down his crane*
platform, holding LV *tightly. A tighter shot sees them descending*
in the spray which creates a rainbow effect.

90

INT. MR BOO'S CLUB. NIGHT

RAY: 'It's over!
    All the rainbows in the sky'
    Over the bloody rainbow, eh?
    'Start to weep, then say goodbye'
    Good fucking bye.
    BOO *nods reassuringly to the audience.*
RAY: 'I won't be seeing rainbows, any more . . .'

EXT. SHIPLEY STREET. NIGHT.
MARI *forces her way past the staggered* SADIE *as they charge
out into the street to see next door on fire, but being doused by
several hoses from the fire engines. She is held back by*
FIREMEN.

RAY (*off*): 'But you'll see lonely sunsets after all.
    It's over it's over it's over! . . .'
MARI: LV LV! LV MY BABY!!!
FIREMAN: It's all right, love – everyone's out.

INT. MR BOO'S CLUB. NIGHT.
*As the living-room window explodes and a fireball crashes
through the Hoff house windows, we cut to* RAY *as he reaches a
huge anguished climax.*

RAY: '. . . It's OOO-VER!!'
    *The audience is silent. He looks at them. Puts the mike
    back. Leans his tired bruised head on it. It makes a thud
    that echoes in the hushed stunned auditorium.* MR BOO
    puts a sympathetic hand on his shoulder but RAY *pushes it
    away nastily.* MR BOO *pats him on his back as he leaves,
    then starts the mission to salvage the show.*

91

MR BOO: The adorable Mr Ray Say, there, ladies and gents
and a little song about his career in showbusiness called
'It's Over'.

EXT. OPEN-AIR THEATRE. SEAFRONT. NIGHT.
LV *sits on the stage in an empty open-air theatre on the seafront.*
BILLY *clunks the lights on and wanders towards her with a spare*
jacket.

BILLY: There you go.
LV: Thanks, Billy.
BILLY: Oh, you're all right, it's just an old one from the van.
LV: Nn . . . no, I mean . . . thanks for getting me out.
BILLY: Oh that's all right.
(*Tries a joke for the first time:*) Hey, you should get out
more often.
It doesn't really work. He looks around at the auditorium
full of deckchairs.
W . . . why did you want to come down here?
LV: Me dad used to bring me here.
Listen to concerts.
BILLY: (*breathes a silent sigh and decides to give it a go*): LV
. . . there's people . . . other than your dad, you
know . . .
Other people . . . well, other people . . . who might . . .
who might think something of you . . .
People who are . . . well . . . still . . . alive.
LV: (*a sudden panic, she gets up and runs off*): Billy . . . I've
got to go.
BILLY: LV??
But she has gone.
(*He mutters to himself.*) Didn't handle that very well.

INT. CHARRED DOWNSTAIRS SHOP. NIGHT.

The door creaks open and LV *creeps in. She staggers in the dark. Shocked by the extent of the damage, she suddenly fears the worst about her own records and rushes on up through the dark stairs.*

INT. CHARRED HOUSE. NIGHT.

The camera goes with LV *all the way through the black house and up to her landing. When she reaches the top, she is shocked out of her shoes by* MARI, *face to face.* MARI, *mascara-stained scary, shines her torch hard in* LV*'s face, forcing her back down the stairs.*

MARI: What happened eh? What happened here then?

    The little match girl who goes burning everything down then?

    The little stick that *wrecks everything!*

    I can't start again, can I, now? . . . I'm too beat.

    Who'd want me anyways, eh? Who'd want me?

    Grabs her, round the neck.

    WHO'D WANT ME?!!

    Suddenly calms, but becomes more sinister, a weird smile.

    Wait a minute . . . What you want anyway?

    Oh, I know . . . your records.

    Well, all the salvage crap's out on the back roof, LV.

    Maybe they'll be there.

    Lets go. LV *runs out through the kitchen . . .*

EXT. BACK ROOF. HOUSE. NIGHT.

. . . and on to the back roof, which is a sea of broken shards of old record, street light glinting off them. She stops suddenly, as if breath has been taken from her. She sees the smashed picture of her dad among the debris. Stunned, severely wounded, she gently picks up a piece of broken record. She opens her mouth to scream

but nothing comes out. Opens it again. Nothing. MARI *appears behind her. Whispers nastily.*

MARI: What's up? Cat got your tongue?
> LV *goes for* MARI, *violently, forcefully. She gets hold of her chin with one hand and holds the sharp curved shard of record to her throat with the other, and marches her round the roof.* LV*'s hands leave black marks over* MARI*'s face. Words rush out, pouring out, loud, like we've never heard her before.*

LV: Aaaaa! Aaaaa! Can you hear me now, mother?
> My dad . . . You drove him as fast as you could to an
> early grave with your men and your shouting and your
> pals and your nights, and your nights, and your nights,
> and your nights, and your nights of *neglect.*
> Oh, when he had his records on . . . he sparkled, not
> dazzling like you, but with fine lights . . . *fine* lights!
> He never spoke up to you, 'cos you would never listen
> . . . And I never spoke up to you . . .
> 'COS I COULD NEVER GET A WORD IN!!
> MARI *recoils from the enormous noise.*

EXT. BAY/TOWN. NIGHT.
The echo of LV*'s scream drifts over the town. Dogs start to bark.*

EXT. BACK ROOF. HOUSE. NIGHT.
MARI *is still reeling from the vocal gale.*

MARI (*stunned*): Little Voice . . . ?
LV: (*walks away and leaves her*): My name's Laura.

EXT. PIGEON HILL. DAWN.

As dawn breaks, BILLY *is tending to his birds, especially Duane.*
He senses a presence behind him, turns, and sees LV. *He smiles*
warmly.

BILLY: Everything all right?

LV: Fine. Is that Duane?

BILLY: Yeah, just about back to normal, I reckon.

LV: Aye . . . Reckon I know how he feels.

   They look at each other. LV *smiles.*

BILLY: Hey, you want to give us a hand? With exercise?

LV: All right . . .

   They smile once more.

    Cut to:

    BILLY *shooing off his pigeons out of the coup.* LV *helps*
him, laughing at the mayhem. They fly past her. BILLY
hands her a pigeon which she turns and releases. As she
does so, we freeze-frame on LV *and the bird.*

    END.

CREDITS AND CAST LIST

Miramax Films and Scala present
Little Voice

Directed by	MARK HERMAN
Produced by	ELIZABETH KARLSEN
Screenplay by	MARK HERMAN
Executive Producers	STEPHEN WOOLLEY
	NIK POWELL
Co-executive Producers	BOB WEINSTEIN
	HARVEY WEINSTEIN
	PAUL WEBSTER
Co-producer	LAURIE BORG
Director of Photography	ANDY COLLINS
Production Designer	DON TAYLOR
Editor	MICHAEL ELLIS A.C.E.
Music Supervisor	BOB LAST
Original Music and Arrangements by	JOHN ALTMAN
Costume Designer	LINDY HEMMING

Based on the stage play *The Rise and Fall of Little Voice*
by JIM CARTWRIGHT

Cast in order of appearance

Mari	BRENDA BLETHYN
LV	JANE HORROCKS
Billy	EWAN McGREGOR
George	PHILIP JACKSON
Sadie	ANNETTE BADLAND
Ray Say	MICHAEL CAINE
Mr Boo	JIM BROADBENT

The Bouncers	ADAM FOGERTY
	JAMES WELSH
Stripper	KAREN GREGORY
Arthur	FRED FEAST
LV's Dad	GRAHAM TURNER
Pawnbroker	GEORGE OLIVER
Loan Adviser	VIRGIL TRACY
Money Lender	DICK VAN WINKLE

Mr Boo's Band

GEORGE BRADLEY	GEOFFREY EMMERSON
BARRY GOMERSALT	ANGELA HARRISON
JEAN HOTTON	DAVID KEMP
AIDEN LAWRENCE	MICHAEL LYNSKEY
PETER MARSHALL	PETER MINNS
CHRISTINE QUICK	LEN RANGELY
BOB SCOTT	MELANIE SIMPSON
DOUG STEWART	PETER THOMSON
STAN WRIGHT	

Talent Scout	HOWARD GRACE
Bunnie Morris	ALEX NORTON
George's Girlfriend	MELODIE SCALES

Take Fat

SEAN HADLAND	ROGER NEVILLE
MICHAEL PRIOR	PAUL SWAN
CARL WHITTAKER	

Brenda Bailey	KITTY ROBERTS
Wild Trigger Smith	FRED GAUNT
Elaine	ALITA PETROF
Fireman	JONATHAN CLARK

Casting Director	PRISCILLA JOHN
Sound Recordist	PETER LINDSAY
Unit Production Manager	TONY CLARKSON
Prod. Co-ord./ Post-Prod. Supervisor	WENDY BROOM
Script Supervisor	ANGELA WHARTON
1st Assistant Director	JONATHAN BENSON
Camera Operator	CHRIS PLEVIN
Chief Make-Up & Hair	PETER KING
Production Accountant	KEVIN TREHY
Location Manager	MARK HERBERT
Construction Manager	STEVE BOHAN
Gaffer	CHUCK FINCH
Special Effects Supervisor	BOB HOLLOW
Production Assistant	TANYA FREEDMAN
Producer's/Director's Assistants	ROMANY TURNER
	JEZ THIERRY
Production Runner	RYAN GREEN
Production Liaison – London	RACHAEL COWARD
2nd Assistant Director	SARA DESMOND
3rd Assistant Director	EMMA GRIFFITHS
Crowd Assistant Director	FIONA RICHARDS
Floor Runner (Scarborough)	GRENVILLE BARTLETT
Additional Crowd Assistant Directors	TEAN BORG
	MICK WARD
Focus Puller	MARK MILSOME
Clapper Loader	HARRY BOWERS
Camera Grip	MALCOLM SHEEHAN
Camera Trainee	ELIZABETH TROTT

Steadicam Operator	ADRIAN SMITH
Sound Maintenance	MALCOLM ROSE
Sound Assistant	STEVE FINN
Assistant Costume Designer	NIGEL EGERTON
Wardrobe Supervisor	JENNY HAWKINS
Wardrobe Assistant	DAVID CROSSMAN
Wardrobe Dresser	JIM SMITH
Make-Up/Hair Assistants	TAMSIN DORLING
	KIRSTIE STANWAY
Casting Assistant	ORLA PULTON
Mr Boo's Band Casting	TONY TURNER
Singing Coach	JO THOMPSON
Dialect Coach	PATSY RODENBURG
Assistant Accountant	KATHY EWINGS
Accounts Assistant	CLAIRE ROBERTSON
Location Assistants	ALISON PITMAN
	MARTIN RAINE
1st Assistant Editor	SIMON HARRIS
2nd Assistant Editor	JANE WINKLES
Supervising Sound Editor	RODNEY GLENN
Foley Editor	JONATHAN ENRAGHT-MOONY
Dialogue Editors	TWYDOR DAVIS
	JASON ADAMS
Music Editor	ANDY GLEN
Assistant to Music Editor	TONY LEWIS
Preview Sound	DENNIS McTAGGART
Re-Recording Mixers	RAY MERRIN
	GRAHAM DANIEL
Recordist	LYLE SCOTT-DARLING
Foley/ADR Mixer	ED COLYER

Technical Delivery Co-ordinator	STEPHEN LAW
Supervising Art Director	JO GRAYSMARK
Set Decorator	JOHN BUSH
Construction Art Director	PAUL WESTACOTT
Stand-by Art Director	FRANCES BENNETT
Art Department Runners	JULIE HORAN
	INGE LOEFFEN
Property Master	LES BENSON
Stand-by Props	JOE DIPPLE
	COLIN ELLIS
Prop Storeman	JOHN PALMER
Dressing Props	NEIL MURRUM
	ERIC STRANGE
Stills Photographer	LAURIE SPARHAM
Additional Stills	JOTH SHAKERLEY
Unit Publicist	UNDINE MARSHFIELD
	for WARREN COWAN/
	PHIL SYMES & ASSOCS.
Choreographer	BRUNO TONIOLI
Unit Nurses	NICKY JARVIS
	MICHAEL PRIOR
Stand-ins	JOAN FIELD
	HOWARD GRACE
	BEVERLEY LACEY
	JOHN RUDDY
	REG TURNER
Supervising Carpenter	TOM MARTIN
Supervising Painter	GARY CROSBY
Stand-by Carpenter	CHARLIE GAYNER
Stand-by Painter	PETER WILKINSON
Stand-by Rigger	STEVEN POLLECUTT

Stagehands	MARK GOODMAN
	DEREK WHORLOW
Carpenters	EDDIE BOLGER
	GARY HEDGES
	JOHN O'REGAN
	DANNY O'REGAN JNR.
	PETER WILKINSON
Painters	WILLIAM BROWN
	DEAN DUNHAM
	DAVID HABERFIELD
	PETER PRENTICE
Chargehand Rigger	PETER HAWKINS
Best Boy	BILLY MERRELL
Electricians	SAM BLOOR
	MARK 'GIFFER' EVANS
	STEVE FINCH
Genny Operator	GEORGE WORLEY
Electrical Labourer	ROBERT TOMLINSON
Special Effects Assistants	PAUL CLAYTON
	SIMON DAVEY
	ADAM HOLLOW
Digital Effects Producer	CRAIG CHANDLER
Stunt Co-ordinator	LEE SHEWARD
Stunt Doubles	JIM DOWDALL
	JAMIE EDGEHILL
	MARK HENSON
Foley Artists	PAULINE GRIFFITHS
	JENNY LEE-WRIGHT
Unit Drivers	PETER BROOK
	BARRY NEWELL
	COLIN MORRIS
	STEVE TIMMS
	MAGGIE LODGE

Minibus Drivers	ADRIAN GOLDY
	ALEX ROBINSON
	PAULA ADAMSON
Transport Captain	HUGH McLELLAN

Facilities Drivers

MICK CROWLEY	ROBERT DIXON
TOM INNES	ROSS KEEL
DEAN MACEY	IAN MASKELL
NICK SMALLEY	DENIS SWAN
ROY TAIT	PETER THOMPSON
RICKY TITCOMBE	KEITH WEST
DALE WILSON	

Miramax Production Executive	LAURA MADDEN
Miramax Legal and Business Affairs	ISABEL BEGG
Scala Business Affairs	STEVE ZIELINSKI
Assistant to Stephen Woolley	PHILIPPA WOOD
Assistant to Nik Powell	SUE CARRECK
Scala Accountant	JOHN MORGAN

Second Unit Additional Photography

Production Manager	WENDY BROOM
Lighting Cameraman	IAN WILSON
Camera Operator	ROGER McDONALD
Focus Pullers	MIKE GREEN
	JONATHAN SYKES
Clapper Loaders	CHRIS BAINES
	JACKIE OUDNEY
Camera Grip	GARY HUTCHINS
Location Manager	PIP SHORT
Script Supervisor	CATHY DOUBLEDAY
2nd Assistant Director	ANTONY FORD

3rd Assistant Director	TREVOR WRIGHT
Wardrobe Assistant	VANESSA MUNRO
Accountant	ANN SHIELDS
Best Boy	WARREN EWEN
Electricians	GARY COLKETT
	ABBIE EWING
	WICK FINCH
Genny Operator	MICKY JAMES
Drivers	PETER NEWSON
	NEIL PEARSON

Suppliers

Action Vehicles	TLO
Camera Consumables	THE FILM GAME
Camera Cranes	PANAVISION
	MANCHESTER
	TECHNOVISION
	CAMERAS LTD.
Catering	MOBILE MOUTHFUL
Cherrypickers	NATIONWIDE SKYLIFT
Color by	DELUXE LONDON
Computer Services	SARGENT-DISC LTD.,
	LONDON
Costume Hire	ANGELS AND BERMANS
Film and Digital Opticals by	GENERAL SCREEN
	ENTERPRISES
	FILM & DIGITAL
	EFFECTS STUDIOS
Health and Safety	H&S ADVISORY
	SERVICE
Insurance Services	AON/ALBERT G RUBEN
Legal Services	OLSWANG
Lighting Equipment	LEE LIGHTING
supplied by	LIMITED
Low Loader	BICKERS ACTION

Pigeons supplied by	PROP FARM LTD.
	PETER THORPE
Post Production Facilities	GOLDCREST POST
	PRODUCTION
Post Production Script	SAPEX SCRIPTS
Re-recorded at	SHEPPERTON SOUND
ADR Loop Group	BRENDAN DONNISON -
	LYPS INC.
Sound Playback Equipment	F.A.B. SOUND SERVICES
	RICHMOND FILM
	SERVICES
Telecine Facilities	VIDFILM EUROPE
Titles by	CAPITAL FX (LONDON)
Transport supplied by	ON SET LOCATION
	SERVICES
	LAYS INTERNATIONAL
	PICK-UPS TRANSPORT
	PRACTICAL CAR & VAN
	RENTAL
	MITCHELLS SELF
	DRIVE
Travel Services	THE TRAVEL
	COMPANY
TV Playback	RON OSMAN
Walkie Talkies	AUDIOLINK LTD.

With Special Thanks to
JACK LECHNER, KEVIN HYMAN, JOHN HADITY,
GINETTE CHALMERS, TIM CORRIE, LINDY KING,
HARRIET ROBINSON, SALLY LONG-INNES,
DEBORAH HARWOOD, DAVID AUKIN,
ALLON REICH, TERRY LANSBURY, IAN ROBINSON,
MIKE STAINER, JASON WHEELER and Team,
FINOLA DWYER, JONATHAN KARLSEN,
AMANDA POSEY, RACHEL WOOD, LUCY RYAN,

ANNE McNULTY, OLIVIA STEWART,
RACHEL CHARTRES, PAUL COWAN,
Staff at ST. NICHOLAS HOTEL, WREAHEAD HOTEL
and EAST AYTON LODGE,
BRITISH TELECOMMUNICATIONS PLC.,
NORTH YORKSHIRE POLICE
(SCARBOROUGH DEPARTMENT),
SCARBOROUGH BOROUGH COUNCIL,
SOUTH BAY TRADERS ASSOCIATION,
HAVEN HOLIDAYS (CAYTON BAY),
STEPHEN JOSEPH THEATRE,
The people of SCARBOROUGH, and JOY,
HARVEY and LAURA HERMAN.

Original Stage Production Directed by SAM MENDES

Music Co-ordinator	HEATHER BOWNASS
Music Recorded and Mixed at	ANGEL RECORDING STUDIOS - LONDON CTS STUDIOS LANSDOWNE STUDIOS
Engineered by	STEVE PRICE
Assisted by	TOM JENKINS
Music Fixer	ISOBEL GRIFFITHS

109

110

Performed by Jane Horrocks
Arranged by John Altman

'SING AS WE GO'
Written by Harry Parr-Davies
Published by Francis Day & Hunter Limited
Performed by Jane Horrocks
Arranged by John Altman

'TUB THUMPING'
Written by Alice Nutter/Louise Watts/
Judith Abbot/Nigel Hunter/Darren Hammer/
Allan Whalley/Paul Greco/Dunstan Bruce
Published by EMI Music Publishing Limited
Performed by Chumbawamba
Courtesy of EMI Elecrola GmbH
by arrangement of EMI Records

'RAWHIDE'
Written by Ned Washington & Dimitri Tiomkin
Courtesy of Largo Music Inc/Patti Washington Music/
Volta Music Corp
Administered by BMG Music Publishing Ltd.
Performed by Frankie Laine
Courtesy of Columbia Records/
Sony Music Entertainment UK Ltd.
by arrangement with Sony Music Licensing

Excerpt from
'I NEVER CRIED SO MUCH
IN ALL MY LIFE'
By Haines/Harper/Castling
Copyright 1936 Campbell Connelly Co. Ltd.

113

METHUEN SCREENPLAYS

☐ BEAUTIFUL THING	Jonathan Harvey	£6.99
☐ THE ENGLISH PATIENT	Anthony Minghella	£7.99
☐ THE CRUCIBLE	Arthur Miller	£6.99
☐ THE WIND IN THE WILLOWS	Terry Jones	£7.99
☐ PERSUASION	Jane Austen, adapted by Nick Dear	£6.99
☐ TWELFTH NIGHT	Shakespeare, adapted by Trevor Nunn	£7.99
☐ THE KRAYS	Philip Ridley	£7.99
☐ THE AMERICAN DREAMS (THE REFLECTING SKIN & THE PASSION OF DARKLY NOON)	Philip Ridley	£8.99
☐ MRS BROWN	Jeremy Brock	£7.99
☐ THE GAMBLER	Dostoyevsky, adapted by Nick Dear	£7.99
☐ TROJAN EDDIE	Billy Roche	£7.99
☐ THE WINGS OF THE DOVE	Hossein Amini	£7.99
☐ THE ACID HOUSE TRILOGY	Irvine Welsh	£8.99
☐ THE LONG GOOD FRIDAY	Barrie Keeffe	£6.99
☐ SLING BLADE	Billy Bob Thornton	£7.99

• All Methuen Drama books are available through mail order or from your local bookshop.

Please send cheque/eurocheque/postal order (sterling only) Access, Visa, Mastercard, Diners Card, Switch or Amex.

☐☐☐☐☐☐☐☐☐☐☐☐☐☐☐☐

Expiry Date:_____ Signature: _____

Please allow 75 pence per book for post and packing U.K.
Overseas customers please allow £1.00 per copy for post and packing.

ALL ORDERS TO:

Methuen Books, Books by Post, TBS Limited, The Book Service, Colchester Road, Frating Green, Colchester, Essex CO7 7DW.

NAME: _____

ADDRESS: _____

_____

_____

Please allow 28 days for delivery. Please tick box if you do not
wish to receive any additional information ☐

Prices and availability subject to change without notice.

A SELECTED LIST OF
METHUEN MODERN PLAYS

☐	CLOSER	Patrick Marber	£6.99
☐	THE BEAUTY QUEEN OF LEENANE	Martin McDonagh	£6.99
☐	A SKULL IN CONNEMARA	Martin McDonagh	£6.99
☐	THE LONESOME WEST	Martin McDonagh	£6.99
☐	THE CRIPPLE OF INISHMAAN	Martin McDonagh	£6.99
☐	THE STEWARD OF CHRISTENDOM	Sebastian Barry	£6.99
☐	SHOPPING AND F***ING	Mark Ravenhill	£6.99
☐	FAUST (FAUST IS DEAD)	Mark Ravenhill	£5.99
☐	POLYGRAPH	Robert Lepage and Marie Brassard	£6.99
☐	BEAUTIFUL THING	Jonathan Harvey	£6.99
☐	MEMORY OF WATER & FIVE KINDS OF SILENCE	Shelagh Stephenson	£7.99
☐	WISHBONES	Lucinda Coxon	£6.99
☐	BONDAGERS & THE STRAW CHAIR	Sue Glover	£9.99
☐	SOME VOICES & PALE HORSE	Joe Penhall	£7.99
☐	KNIVES IN HENS	David Harrower	£6.99
☐	BOYS' LIFE & SEARCH AND DESTROY	Howard Korder	£8.99
☐	THE LIGHTS	Howard Korder	£6.99
☐	SERVING IT UP & A WEEK WITH TONY	David Eldridge	£8.99
☐	INSIDE TRADING	Malcolm Bradbury	£6.99
☐	MASTERCLASS	Terrence McNally	£5.99
☐	EUROPE & THE ARCHITECT	David Grieg	£7.99
☐	BLUE MURDER	Peter Nichols	£6.99
☐	BLASTED & PHAEDRA'S LOVE	Sarah Kane	£7.99

• All Methuen Drama books are available through mail order or from your local bookshop.

Please send cheque/eurocheque/postal order (sterling only) Access, Visa, Mastercard, Diners Card, Switch or Amex.

☐☐☐☐☐☐☐☐☐☐☐☐☐☐☐☐

Expiry Date:_____ Signature: _____

Please allow 75 pence per book for post and packing U.K.
Overseas customers please allow £1.00 per copy for post and packing.

ALL ORDERS TO:

Methuen Books, Books by Post, TBS Limited, The Book Service, Colchester Road, Frating Green, Colchester, Essex CO7 7DW.

NAME: _____

ADDRESS: _____

_____

_____

Please allow 28 days for delivery. Please tick box if you do not wish to receive any additional information ☐

Prices and availability subject to change without notice.

METHUEN DRAMA
MONOLOGUE & SCENE BOOKS

☐ CONTEMPORARY SCENES FOR ACTORS (MEN)	Earley and Keil	£8.99
☐ CONTEMPORARY SCENES FOR ACTORS (WOMEN)	Earley and Keil	£8.99
☐ THE CLASSICAL MONOLOGUE (MEN)	Earley and Keil	£7.99
☐ THE CLASSICAL MONOLOGUE (WOMEN)	Earley and Keil	£7.99
☐ THE CONTEMPORARY MONOLOGUE (MEN)	Earley and Keil	£7.99
☐ THE CONTEMPORARY MONOLOGUE (WOMEN)	Earley and Keil	£7.99
☐ THE MODERN MONOLOGUE (MEN)	Earley and Keil	£7.99
☐ THE MODERN MONOLOGUE (WOMEN)	Earley and Keil	£7.99
☐ THE METHUEN AUDITION BOOK FOR MEN	Annika Bluhm	£6.99
☐ THE METHUEN AUDITION BOOK FOR WOMEN	Annika Bluhm	£6.99
☐ THE METHUEN AUDITION BOOK FOR YOUNG ACTORS	Anne Harvey	£6.99
☐ THE METHUEN BOOK OF DUOLOGUES FOR YOUNG ACTORS	Anne Harvey	£6.99

• All Methuen Drama books are available through mail order or from your local bookshop.

Please send cheque/eurocheque/postal order (sterling only) Access, Visa, Mastercard, Diners Card, Switch or Amex.

☐☐☐☐☐☐☐☐☐☐☐☐☐☐☐☐

Expiry Date:_____Signature: _____

Please allow 75 pence per book for post and packing U.K.
Overseas customers please allow £1.00 per copy for post and packing.

ALL ORDERS TO:

Methuen Books, Books by Post, TBS Limited, The Book Service, Colchester Road, Frating Green, Colchester, Essex CO7 7DW.

NAME:_____

ADDRESS:_____

_____

Please allow 28 days for delivery. Please tick box if you do not
wish to receive any additional information ☐

Prices and availability subject to change without notice.

Methuen Contemporary Dramatists
include

Peter Barnes (three volumes)
Sebastian Barry
Edward Bond (six volumes)
Howard Brenton
  (two volumes)
Richard Cameron
Jim Cartwright
Caryl Churchill (two volumes)
Sarah Daniels (two volumes)
David Edgar (three volumes)
Dario Fo (two volumes)
Michael Frayn (two volumes)
Peter Handke
Jonathan Harvey
Declan Hughes
Terry Johnson
Bernard-Marie Koltès
Doug Lucie
David Mamet (three volumes)

Anthony Minghella
  (two volumes)
Tom Murphy (four volumes)
Phyllis Nagy
Peter Nichols (two volumes)
Philip Osment
Louise Page
Stephen Poliakoff
  (three volumes)
Christina Reid
Philip Ridley
Willy Russell
Ntozake Shange
Sam Shepard (two volumes)
David Storey (three volumes)
Sue Townsend
Michel Vinaver (two volumes)
Michael Wilcox

For a Complete Catalogue of Methuen Drama titles
write to:

Methuen Drama
20 Vauxhall Bridge Road
London SW1V 2SA